The Entrepren

TELEMARKETING THAT WORKS

How To Create A Winning Program For Your Company

Raymond
C. Harlan &
Walter M.
Woolfson, Jr.

PROBUS PUBLISHING COMPANY
Chicago, Illinois

This publication is designed to provide accurate and authoritative information in regard to the subject matter covered. It is sold with the understanding that the publisher is not engaged in rendering legal, accounting or other professional service. If legal or other expert assistance is required, the services of a competent professional should be sought.

Library of Congress Cataloging in Publication Data Available.

ISBN   1-55738-203-4

Printed in the United States of America

IPC

1   2   3   4   5   6   7   8   9   0

*This book is dedicated to Dee, without whom it
would never have come to be.*

TABLE OF CONTENTS

PREFACE

Every increase in postal rates, every jump in the price of gas pushes more managers into a reappraisal of telemarketing. As direct mail and traveling sales programs become more costly, telemarketing becomes more attractive. More and more managers are looking at the telephone, not as an adjunct to other marketing strategies, but as the primary means to move the product and stay attuned to customers' needs.

As the tide of telemarketing swelled in the last decade, so did the list of telemarketing books. So why write another one?

We found a number of books telling the reader how to sell over the phone. While this book also covers that topic, we wanted it to do more. We set out to write an affordable book which described how to set up a successful telemarketing program. We felt managers needed a book which would describe all aspects of the process. The result is more than a book about selling: it describes how to hire and train good people and how to keep them from burning out; how to integrate direct mail and phone calls; how to calculate the cost of different approaches; how to set up an effective record-keeping system, and more.

More than anything else, we wanted a book which gave marketing its proper due. Used properly, the telephone is more than a selling tool. With alert, trained callers, the phone is the best possible means for gaining crucial information about customer needs—information that can spark changes in promotional methods or even the product itself. Best of all, this marketing information accumulates while sales are being made.

The broader approach of this book should have a special appeal to four types of people:

1. A manager or owner looking for cost-effective ways to expand the company's current marketing efforts.

2. Anyone wondering about alternatives to present marketing strategies. Is there really a viable alternative to direct mail and a traveling sales force?

3. Anyone whose current telemarketing effort seems haphazard.

4. Anyone wanting to know what's behind the rising excitement over telemarketing.

The speed, flexibility, and low cost of the telephone make it an ideal tool for the fast-changing marketplace of the 90's—if it is matched with quick-thinking, flexible managers. Therein lies the challenge.

Raymond C. Harlan

ACKNOWLEDGEMENTS

The final form of this book owes a great deal to a number of people. The most obvious of these is Walter's widow, Dee Woolfson. At Walter's death, he left behind a disordered mound of papers. Without Dee's determination, the idea for a book would have died at that point.

My father, Ross Harlan, and my friend and colleague, Gary Gaessler, read the manuscript and suggested a number of changes to strengthen it.

In this project I discovered anew that writing can be a lonely and frustrating task. Throughout it all, my wife Linda was a constant source of strength—celebrating our victories, lending encouragement when I was down, and showing extraordinary patience when I became withdrawn and edgy.

Thanks to all.

Ray Harlan

CHAPTER 1

TELEMARKETING: THE MANAGER'S PERSPECTIVE

THE BENEFITS OF TELEMARKETING

By all accounts telephone use in sales campaigns is expanding dramatically. Even the traditional Girl Scout cookie campaigns are being updated as older girls learn sophisticated telemarketing skills to complement the established door-to-door techniques. One Girl Scout council in California reports a 28% sales increase through the addition of telephone techniques including a toll-free 800 number (*The Denver Post*, 4 March 1990, p. 4G).

One reason for the rapid growth of telemarketing in the last two decades is easy to see. Rapidly evolving technology has drawn attention to the field. For organizations willing to make the investment, machines can now take over much of the tedium associated with the business telephone. A machine can call numbers from a list; screen no-answers, busy signals, and answering machines; and finally present the marketer with an information screen matched to a live human being on the phone. After the prospect is convinced, the telemarketer can tap a couple of keys and the system will send an order to the shipping department and prepare an invoice.

Technology has also taken away the traditional advantage of direct mail in putting printed material directly into a prospect's hands. A telephone coupled with a fax machine can get a price sheet or product specifications from Miami to Melbourne faster than direct mail can get it across town. A newer development, interactive fax, automatically sends back specific information in response to a faxed request. Customers and prospects are happy because they can get information almost instantaneously. The telemarketing staff, being freed from processing routine information requests, can concentrate on servicing and developing high-value accounts.

Although advancing technology has spurred the growth of telemarketing, the new machines actually only leverage the telephone's traditional advantages. The telephone's advantages in marketing have always been personal contact at low cost and unmatched flexibility. As postal rates, air fares, and gasoline prices climb, contacts by phone become relatively less expensive. According to a telemarketing industry publication, the average cost of a face-to-face sales call is $291.15 (*INBOUND/OUTBOUND*, Feb. 1989, p. 3).

While a phone call does not offer all the elements of a face-to-face meeting, it does allow the caller to adjust to the customer's needs. That flexibility in responding to the customer, coupled with the inherently low cost per contact, is what gives telemarketing its power.

Flexibility is available on a wider scale as well. Telemarketing allows an astute manager to make mid-course corrections during a sales campaign. If the first hundred or the first thousand calls in a campaign turn up unexpected results, a manager can suspend operations and make changes in the sales approach, or the calling lists, or even the product. By contrast, a campaign based on direct mail or electronic or print advertising, if it is off-target, may soak up vast resources before corrections can be made.

A smart marketing director can, of course, hedge bets by limiting a mail or advertising campaign to one city or one industry. The problem comes when test marketing results are disappointing or inconclusive. Everyone can see the program is off-track, but what needs to be changed? In a well-designed telemarketing campaign, callers will not only attempt to sell products, they will also collect information from people who don't buy—information that is critical in making mid-course corrections. The same information can be gathered face-to-face, of course, but much more slowly and at higher cost.

To make the most effective use of the telephone, either alone or in conjunction with other approaches, a manager must constantly be alert for opportunities to exploit the unique advantages of the telephone:

1. Low cost personal contact.

2. Flexibility in responding to customer needs.

3. Flexibility in adjusting the sales campaign.

What complicates the picture is fear—on the part of the manager, the sales and marketing staff, or other company principals.

THE FEAR OF TELEMARKETING

Telephone Resistance: Ironically, in an information age based on sophisticated technology, the phone—the oldest high technology tool used in marketing and sales—is often misunderstood, misused, abused, and even ignored by some of the men and woman who manage marketing and selling programs.

Why should an instrument that repeatedly proves its value in low-cost, high-profit, top-volume sales programs be resisted by sales and marketing departments in companies that could increase both market shares and profits by strategically managed telemarketing programs?

There is no simple answer to this question. A broad range of factors tend to downgrade the telephone in the minds of many managers who could use it, alone or in combination with other tools, more effectively than they currently use a traveling sales force or other methods.

Whenever telemarketing is rarely used or isn't achieving its potential as a marketing/sales technique, the failure can usually be traced to a manager who doesn't understand its possibilities, or who is simply prejudiced against the telephone.

Personality Factors: What are the factors in a manager's personality and experience that cause him or her to insist that "the company cannot use a telephone to make sales" or "telemarketing doesn't fit our image"? Some are commonplace. Managers, like everyone else, tend to blame the telephone for a variety of bad actions that only human beings are capable of performing. It is the telephone that invaded our privacy when a marketing person phoned on a Saturday to pester us with personal questions ranging from our investment plans to whether we prefer sail boats or cabin cruisers. And when we said we didn't have time to answer questions, the interviewer got brassy. It was the telephone that tried to gyp our grandparents out of their life savings.

When we have to phone somebody to ask marketing questions or present a product, it is the telephone that hangs up on us, rejects us in a thousand ways, and kills our sales. And, of course, it is the telephone which gave birth to a litter of answering devices that block talk with real people who fail to call us back.

It also is the phone that cuts into our business day, interrupts our favorite TV programs when we're at home, and sometimes shrieks us awake at 3 a.m. only to let us know that the party at the other end didn't want us in the first place. We have to expect a certain amount of irritability connected with the phone, but the resistance of some managers runs deeper.

Historical Factors: Selling was being conducted successfully in the United States long before Alexander Graham Bell patented the telephone in 1876. As a product the phone went through a novelty period. Then for several decades it was a social instrument with some minor business overtones. In those days travel was cheaper; long-distance phone calls were expensive, time-consuming, and unreliable; and telegrams offered comparable speed and better message quality. The cult of the traveling salesman was born as the real "Willy Lohmans" and "Music Men" traveled the narrow highways and the rails convinced that face-to-face contact was the key to sales.

Tradition and Inertia: Much of the prejudice against telemarketing comes from the entrenched habits of successful sales people. They think about the telephone negatively because they are conditioned to go through a complete series of expensive acts before making a sale. Their ritual requires them to see the customers' expressions and body language in order to judge the effectiveness of a proposal or ferret out an issue that might be the pivot for a sale. They are attuned to making plane reservations, filling out expense accounts, sleeping in hotels or motels, taking a lot of travel time from city to city to permit recharging of their batteries, and counting on the reassurance they always get when a customer gives them a half-hour or an hour of valuable time to place an order. These are not necessarily valid reasons for doing business the way it was done when phones had to be cranked, but they can be harder to break than a drug habit.

Against this background, it is little wonder that many sales managers give too much credence to the reasonable, but dated opinions of their traveling representatives: "I can't even sell to my oldest customers unless I can see them and talk with them face to face." "I don't like telephoning. It's too impersonal."

Closely related to the negativism of an outside sales force is the attitude of some sales managers who have told us: "Our sales people have to travel to physically inventory each customer's stock. Our competitors do that and it's the only way to tell what the customers need." But it's no longer the only way. Remote inventory systems offer significant advantages to both buyer and seller.

The Boiler-Room Image: Telephone scams and unprofessional operations have given telephone selling a bad name. Actual boiler rooms are becoming rare as steam heat falls into disuse, but "boiler-room tactics," unfortunately, are flourishing. The North American Securities Administrators Association believes U.S. citizens lose $10 billion a year to investment fraud perpetrated over the phone. That's more than $1 million per hour. (*The Denver Post,* 26 January 1990, p. 1C.)

The same technology which has spurred the boom in legitimate telemarketing has also made it easier to be a successful scam artist. The Alliance Against Fraud in Telemarketing reports some businesses are using 1-900 numbers to charge dollars per minute for information consumers could get for free. In some cases callers are put on hold as the bill keeps climbing.

With the world now largely interconnected electronically, operators set up boiler-rooms off-shore in Costa Rica, Liberia, South Africa and elsewhere. Offering spurious foreign investment schemes, they are immune from prosecution in the U.S. (*The Denver Post*, 26 January 1990, p. 5C.)

Given these circumstances, even the most persuasive marketing director may have an uphill battle to get telemarketing approval from an image-conscious owner or senior vice-president. There's always a good chance that a strong presentation for telemarketing is going to be made on the same day that the final decision-maker has just read about the latest phone scam.

The truth is both businesses and individuals will respond positively to telemarketing if the callers are respectful and adjust to the customers' needs. A manager who wants to build a powerful telemarketing program must always keep in mind the need to distinguish this program from the boiler-room scams. Everything—the design of the product, the hiring of callers, the writing of a calling script or outline, the design of record-keeping and compensation systems—everything should enhance the image of respectability and concern for the customer. We are not here to "take" anyone; we are here to meet the customer's needs.

Telemarketing as an Afterthought: Historically, many companies that have engaged in some form of telemarketing have relegated the program to a secondary role. Hiring for telemarketing frequently has been a careless process; training has been inadequate; compensation systems have encouraged pressure tactics and poor records, and the traveling sales force has gotten more respect. With that approach, the results are predictable: low morale, high turnover, and a boiler-room image in the minds of the customers.

Consider a case in point: an executive in a general investment company wanted to hire and use a small telephone staff for a limited marketing objective—to increase attendance at special seminars that were falling short of his goals. We'll call his company ABC Reliable Brokerage and we'll call him George Bergen, Investment Counselor, although both names are fictitious.

Bergen felt he required a consultant to set up his program and he hired one of the authors. Although he recognized the need for management consultation, he hired a staff of two without screening by the consultant.

In his first conversation with the consultant he said: "I've hired these two gophers. One used to be an employment agency head-hunter, and the other was a magazine subscription solicitor."

Consultant: "What's a 'gopher'?"

Bergen: "You know. It comes from 'go for'! These are people who normally run small errands in our business. They go for the mail, or they go for office supplies, and in this case I'm going to have them go for more prospects on the phone by having them offer invitations to my seminars."

Consultant: "And you're thinking of these people as 'gophers'?"

Bergen: "What's wrong with that. It's a perfectly harmless term, and I'm not going to call them that to their faces."

At that time, in the first months of 1983, he had figured a compensation framework for them of about $175 per week without fringe benefits of any kind. He expected them to work as contractors out of their homes, and he expected them to sign up 30 prospects for his seminars every week for the remainder of the year and beyond without having them quit. If there was ever a losing game plan, this non-sales manager, telemarketing novice had written it.

THE MANAGER'S ROLE
IN TELEMARKETING

Correcting the Afterthought Syndrome: Every manager has to make choices about the efficient use of resources. Compared with face-to-face visits, the telephone offers a very cheap means for personal contact. But in the example above Bergen had tried to make it even cheaper. Had he proceeded as planned, the result would have been low productivity and high turnover.

As it was explained to Bergen, 'gopher' was not a good job description for the work he wanted. These were not school children trying to build a college fund or add to their allowance. He needed experienced professionals who could handle responsibility and operate for long periods with minimal supervision. They needed a strong flair for communicating ideas on the phone and a solid professional attitude, which would give the public a positive image of the company. Without these characteristics, they couldn't possibly use the telephone effectively as a marketing tool. A gopher could not do the job; neither could a professional treated as a gopher.

Fortunately, Bergen was convinced. He dropped the "go for" concept and raised compensation and incentives. The consultant conducted a one-day training program, and together they created a direct-mail follow-up to send after each initial telephone call. The revised program came close to meeting the original goals.

Phone Skills and Management Know-How: Management of telemarketing, like management of anything else, requires general management skills combined with knowledge of the particular operation. George Bergen was an example of an experienced manager with limited knowledge of telemarketing operations. Managers with limited telemarketing experience are susceptible to a number of problems:

1. Establishing unrealistic goals.

2. Pushing high pressure tactics, perhaps by unconscious modeling based on exposure as a customer to the "boiler-room" approach.

3. Writing inflexible, unworkable scripts.

4. Failing to recognize or cope with burnout.

5. Neglecting to collect information systematically.

6. Committing too many resources before testing a concept.

For a manager without telemarketing experience, we recommend two approaches:

1. Hire an experienced telemarketer whose philosophy is compatible with the objectives for the campaign. That person can either run the campaign or serve as an advisor.

2. Participate in the campaign to stay close to the action. By placing some of the phone calls, a manager will gain credibility and have a much better feel for what is working and what isn't.

The opposite problem can also occur. Sometimes the telephone fails as a marketing or sales tool because the manager isn't a qualified manager in the first place. For the same reasons a star baseball player may become a poor club manager, a star on the phone may not function efficiently when in charge of the operation. A person who is strongly self-motivated may not understand how to motivate others. A naturally articulate, outgoing "people person" may not know how to train others in establishing rapport. A consistent sales winner may not know how to deal with the depression of a sales slump.

Someone has said management is the art of getting things done through others. It follows that telemarketing management is the art of getting others to market and sell effectively over the phone.

Getting others to market and sell effectively requires the usual management skills: the ability to concurrently focus on strategic objectives and immediate operations, to spot and correct weaknesses, to allocate resources for maximum efficiency, to stay abreast of rapidly changing conditions, and to enforce standards.

But the strain telemarketing puts on callers requires an extraordinary attention to "people issues." A structural engineer or equipment specialist may be suffering from family troubles at home; but, unless the problems become completely debilitating, the buildings will still stand, and the equipment will get to those who need it. Not so with telemarketing: a caller suffering from domestic trouble can go through all the motions, saying the same words as before, and turn off every prospect by a lame tone of voice.

An effective telemarketing manager must have enough rapport to listen to off-the-job problems and must be close enough to the workers to sense when on-the-job difficulties are creating boredom or frustration. The manager must ensure adequate compensation and training to give people the motivation and skills to do the job. And he or she must be able to demonstrate to each person that his or her personal goals are aligned with company objectives. More than most endeavors, telemarketing depends on people who believe in what they are doing.

If people are confident in their skills and believe that each phone call is crucial to getting what they want from life, the telephone becomes a potent tool for forging success.

KEY POINTS

1. The use of telemarketing is increasing rapidly due to advancing technology and the rising cost of travel.

2. Good telemarketing exploits the telephone's unique advantages:

    a. Low-cost personal contact.

    b. Flexibility in responding to customer needs.

    c. Flexibility in adjusting the sales campaign.

3. Many managers and sales people under-rate telemarketing because of tradition and unpleasant associations.

4. A successful telemarketing operation must employ quality people and treat them well, not as a second-class sales force.

5. A director of telemarketing needs both management skills and telemarketing experience.

6. The unique demands placed on callers make a manager's "people skills" critical to success.

CHAPTER 2

THE MARKETING FUNCTION IN A TELEPHONE CAMPAIGN

TELEMARKETING IS MORE THAN SELLING

If every offer made over the phone were instantly accepted, every telephone staff could concentrate on selling and ignore marketing. (Plus, no one would suffer "phone-selling burnout," and no one would buy this book.) But, in the real world, where offers are frequently refused, where prospects hang up or waste the caller's time, where the cost of every call must be carefully weighed—in the real world, marketing is crucial.

Ask a professor of marketing to define his field and you are likely to get a mouthful. For our purposes, marketing is the research and planning that supports a successful sales campaign. A smart entrepreneur will want to know:

1. Who is likely to buy this product (and who isn't).

2. Where likely buyers are concentrated (geographically, by profession, by income strata, etc.).

3. What it will cost to get access to those who are likely to buy.

4. What methods and arguments are most effective for convincing specific prospects to buy.

Ironically, the exclusion of marketing may be due to past success in sales. Some sales managers are easily swept up by the high sales volume and favorable profit ratios made possible by the telephone. Many who become entrepreneurs or telemarketing managers find selling by phone so easy they never stop to analyze their own successes.

THE FATAL
MISCALCULATION

A person who has experienced great success as an individual telemarketer may place too much emphasis on sales when organizing a telephone staff. Thinking of the telephone as a cheap and all-powerful sales instrument can lead a business principal or marketing manager to pour company resources into an ill-fated project. If management emphasis is strictly on HOW MANY SALES DID WE MAKE TODAY? WHAT WAS OUR GROSS THIS WEEK? WHAT ARE OUR SALES PROJECTIONS?, then a project can be far down the road to ruin before anyone realizes something is wrong.

In that environment, telephone callers are not trained or encouraged to listen sensitively to what their prospects tell them. To make matters even less promising, if they do pick up information that indicates the campaign is off target, they are not encouraged to relay that discouraging news to management.

As an example, a small software distribution company is attempting to sell a bookkeeping package to small- and medium-sized companies in a large metropolitan area. The phone staff makes a vast number of calls with meager results; the manager pushes the staff harder and results continue to decline. With all the pressure on making more calls and more sales, no one tracks the reasons behind rejections. If they did collect that information, that is, if they put some emphasis on marketing as opposed to selling, they might uncover crucial information. Perhaps accounting firms in the area have been highly successful in selling an integral bookkeeping/accounting service. Buying a new bookkeeping program would force a prospect firm to set up a different accounting system and possibly change accountants (unlikely).

OVERCOMING STAFF RESISTANCE

To a new telemarketing manager or account representative with a strong record in sales, "marketing" may lose its distinction. The word telemarketing loses much of its significance as the manager who trains telephone callers for a project sees the words "marketing" and "selling" as synonymous.

The problem is compounded because someone with a good sales personality loves to sell. For a good sales professional, a sale is more than a commission; it is the reason for being. It produces a positive high—excitement at the most elevated pitch the business world can produce. The thrill of making a convincing presentation that leads to a sale is what keeps sales professionals in the business.

Marketing is heavier and duller, and the average sales person whether on the phone, across a desk, or across a counter wants to avoid it. The only exception occurs when *someone else* does the hard research and furnishes results that make it easier to sell and earn commissions.

Telemarketing managers and their staffs need to recognize the marketing half of telemarketing as the foundation for long-term success.

A manager who integrates marketing and sales and defines the telephone staff's value in terms of both functions will lessen staff turnover and burnout when sales start to sag.

MARKETING AND SELLING AS A UNIFIED FUNCTION

In sales jargon the word "qualify" can be used as a verb. To "qualify" a prospect is to determine if the prospect has all the necessary qualifications to make a specific purchase.

Market research attempts to qualify buyers as specifically as possible, and nothing accomplishes this cheaper or faster than a telephone test which combines sales and marketing. A strong selling effort to a sampling of prospects will turn up the numbers by which reasonably accurate sales projections can be made. The same test will reveal objections to the way products and services are constructed, priced, and presented. Changes can then be made before committing further resources.

Even though many managers regard telephone sales representatives exclusively as sellers, members of a telephone staff need to be regarded as marketer/seller personalities and need to be trained that way. As mentioned earlier, these needs pose a serious problem because the work of a market researcher is slow and task-oriented and it takes relatively large amounts of "grunt work" unlikely to appeal to high-powered sales people. In a successful marketing effort, the call report made after each call must be more complex than the simple ordering information taken in a straight sales campaign. Complete records must also be kept of contacts that are utterly negative and worthless as prospects. As you would expect, these requirements can seem like a useless paper mill to people who thrive on selling.

To do effective research without becoming despondent, telephone staffers need to consider the word "no" as a fact to be recorded rather than a personal rejection. Since the word "no" is incompatible with sales, a manager has to help the staff understand the value of digging for objections and negative responses, as comfortably as possible, as they close sales in the selling phase. The staff must understand that a failure in the selling function (no sale) can be a success in the marketing function if it helps focus the campaign.

Every telemarketing office needs a sign that reads: "IF YOU HAVEN'T HEARD THE WORD 'NO' TODAY, YOU HAVEN'T BEEN ON THE PHONE."

The staff should be comfortable with a sliding scale of objectives. The first objective of a call is to make a sale. Should that not be possible, the second objective is to keep the potential transaction open through at least one follow-up mailing and phone call. An absolute turn-down opens the third objective, to acquire critical marketing information.

Burnout and turnover can be reduced for even the least experienced phone sales representatives when the marketing aspect of a phone call is so well accepted by the boss that carefully analyzed and recorded "no" answers have the same importance as immediate sales in reaching long-range objectives. This approach increases satisfaction since a caller succeeds and fails in varying degrees with every call. There is no such thing as a string of failures.

The ability of a well-trained professional staff to operate comfortably in two modes can make telemarketing exceptionally economical. Too often large corporations (and some small ones) run a telephone market research campaign followed by a telephone sales campaign. When it takes two different people to perform the market research function and the selling function, costs of an operation rise dramatically. Also, the lack of unity between the two functions can reduce the validity of market research. Worse, a hostile market can be created by too many calls from the same company. If the team tries to avoid hostility by concealing the name of the company in telephone interviews, desirable sources become distrustful and clam up.

THE FALLACY
OF MARKET SURVEYS

It is one thing to run a telephone marketing survey by having your staff ask a long list of questions that have speculative answers as their objective; it is quite another to test market by "sales" and "no sales."

In speculative marketing surveys, conditional sentences encourage persons being surveyed to answer "yes" to questions they might otherwise answer "no." It's easy to say "yes" when it doesn't cost anything, and "no" is a difficult word for many of us. The data collected by the word "if" is never as finely tuned nor as sharp as what is achieved by the question "Can I have your order?"

As a business person and consumer, you have probably been called by market researchers who are not sales oriented. In consumer-oriented research, they are likely to ask these typical questions:

1. "If you were buying a car today, which make and model would you prefer?" Problem—Sometimes the answer is that although I don't have two dimes jangling in my jeans, I would still prefer a Mercedes with all the options. "If wishes were horses, beggars would ride."

2. "Do you prefer champagne or beer?" Purpose: to establish the purchasing power of the person being interviewed or to narrow the sample to beer drinkers as a means of obtaining numbers on potential sales of a new beer. Problem—People will lie. A beer drinker may answer "champagne" to sound more elegant.

3. "Since I don't have your name, will you tell me your personal income, how big your house is, and how much you spend on ocean cruise vacations each year?" Problem—How does the person being interviewed know that your staffer doesn't have his or her name? Also, in connection with this type of conditional questioning, is there any value to phone numbers without names, and if there is value, isn't it terribly limited?

The number of such questions seems infinite and a business-to-business researcher will have a similar list ("How much do you spend on fax and copier paper in a month?," etc.).

The same sort of data can be collected by mail; although, the reliability is less than with phone interviews because you have no way of knowing why some people do not return the surveys.

Sometimes market survey answers can be compared effectively with data collected in similar fashion over many years by mail and phone interviews. Computers make such comparisons simpler than they were in the pen and pencil era. Even so, conditional questioning and close comparisons of data are a tortuous way for a management team to arrive at an effective sales strategy. If the costs and the time losses in these "first-step-go-nowhere" surveys are hidden in what appears to be a satisfactory sales and profit profile, a telemarketing manager may not realize how much time is lost at the beginning of each sales campaign.

THE BENEFITS OF
A PILOT SALES PROGRAM

A telemarketing team can almost always get better information quicker when the research function involves the acid test of attempted sales to potential customers. While speculative market surveys require guesswork as to prospect's motives, findings derived from pilot program phone sales work are specific.

"Will you purchase?" When enough people in a market segment, a city, a zip code area, or an industry answer "yes" to this question, the entrepreneur knows the potential exists for a successful large-scale sales drive. When too many people answer "no" in the pilot campaign, the entrepreneur knows something has to change, e.g., the target list, the sales pitch, or the product. If the phone staff have taken their marketing function seriously by asking the right questions and keeping detailed call reports, the cause of the failure should be evident.

How many people have to purchase to make a project viable? Obviously, the answer depends on the average cost per sale. In phone sales a key statistic is sometimes given as a calls-per-sale ratio: that is, the total number of calls divided by the total number of sales. Figuring in the caller's salary and commissions divided by the average number of calls per week, plus the cost of overhead and any support mailings will yield a good estimate of the cost per sale. In doing these calculations remember printing costs and long-distance phone charges create economies of scale as the campaign enlarges.

A slightly more sophisticated analysis would look at the average number of calls to reach the key purchaser or decision-maker and the number of repeat calls to that person before a sale is made.

With these fairly simple calculations, it doesn't take a tremendously heavy sampling or a great deal of time to arrive at a success projection.

If the initial sales strategy is close to the mark, a pilot program can pay its own way or even make money. Even a strategy that needs revision may pull in a few sales and lessen the net cash outlay. By contrast, a speculative market survey brings in no money to offset expenses.

Once a telemarketing manager and staff have these statistics available, it isn't difficult to modify the campaign and scale-up by finding additional mailing lists; by using the sales pitches that worked to create additional direct mail letters, brochures, catalogs, and special presentations; and by recognizing and concentrating on high opportunity segments in a market.

Decisions on pricing, service policies, selling strategies, and advertising become easier because the individual elements of the market—the prospects—have been examined and understood.

Telephone marketing programs can vary widely, but they all need to meet one requirement: to measure purchasing interest. The best way to make that measurement is to carry a sales presentation as far as it will go with each phone call.

HOW LEAD FINDERS AND CLOSERS WORK TOGETHER

Although separate marketing surveys and sales campaigns are usually ill-advised, a division of labor between callers who find promising leads (lead finders) and other callers who complete the sale (closers) can work effectively.

If a product is cheap and simple, every person on the telemarketing staff must be able to handle closings. Suppose we were selling a $39.95 audio cassette album directly to middle-class consumers by phone. We need to get a high percentage of sales on the first call or the cost per sale will be too high. First-call sales are relatively easy to close in this case because the product is easy to explain and easy to understand. Every person making calls should be expected to close.

Conversely, a product that is expensive and complex, with qualified prospects hard to find, may require a two-tiered approach. Imagine that we were selling a modular waste-water filtration system designed for industrial sites. Because the system is modular and pre-manufactured, it requires minimal design work and site preparation and is virtually assured of EPA approval.

With a product of this sort, prospects can be elusive. Every large industrial company is not a prospect, only those which need to expand their water filtration capability. Nor is it readily apparent who the decision-maker is (the president? the environmental engineer? the director of civil engineering and construction? the vice-president of manufacturing operations?). To reach a qualified prospect is likely to require a number of fairly mundane phone calls, which can be made by any smart, articulate staffer. When a qualified prospect does turn up, the need for technical expertise is apparent: "Which solvents does the system handle?" "How does it smooth out peak loads?"

In this situation it would not be economical to train every staffer to handle the technical questions. The logical alternative is a staff with a few expert closers and a number of capable lead finders. The key to success is a closely coordinated team effort between lead finders who open sales and sales personnel who close them, with all parties aware of the need to constantly gather marketing information. Somewhere on the organization chart a single manager has to be on top of both functions, or by its own obesity the program will collapse.

In this type of marketing organization, the measurement for effectiveness is the ratio of sales to calls by the closers. Whenever that ratio is unacceptable, the performances of both the lead finders and the closers must be examined. Either the sales approach is not working or the lead finders are failing to distinguish qualified from unqualified prospects. To make such self-examination more effective, the staff should be divided into small teams consisting of lead finders and closers whose performances can be tracked easily.

LEAD FINDERS' TASKS

What lead finders need to produce are completely qualified prospects who have been told enough about a product and who have been asked enough questions to determine their objections. Merely building a list by phone does not qualify prospects. Only the act of taking a list and determining the prospects' ability and willingness to become purchasers justifies a lead finder's position.

A typical lead finder's job description would include these essential tasks:

1. CLEANING UP THE LIST - Business lists are almost as perishable as fruits and vegetables. Telephone calls can determine who is still in a market and who is not. With today's telecommunications technology a lead finder can quickly find out whether a firm has gone out of business, or whether a raw list phone number has been changed. But the job doesn't stop there. If the phone number has changed, is the address the same? A lead finder who asks for a prospect by name from the raw list may discover another required change because someone new is in the position or because the listed executive never was the right person to make the desired purchasing decision. In complex listings involving cross-references to affiliated and subsidiary companies, even more changes in listings must be considered.

2. TALKING WITH THE RIGHT PERSON - A lead by telephone can only become qualified if the lead finder gets information from the horse's mouth. The lead finder may start with the purchasing agent, run through a whole list of department heads and end up with the superintendent of Grounds. The job isn't finished until the lead finder is talking to THE DECISION-MAKER, someone who has the authority to purchase the product. It is crucial that through as many phone calls as it takes, the lead finder concentrates on getting that specific person to answer the phone and then to answer the questions that will determine a qualified buyer.

3. OPENING A SALE - The test of a qualified lead is how the prospect responds to the actual opening of a sale. Every telephone lead finder must carry marketing research through the opening phases of a sale. Whatever is learned in this process should be recorded objectively in a computer or a card file.

(See Chapter Five for information on record keeping.) One opening for a sale consists of a succinct statement in which a superior feature and a specific benefit to the user are described in the first thirty seconds of the call. A pattern of questions should follow without hesitation. Some potential questions: "Have you come across anything like this? Do you think it would save your company money? Is the amortization period attractive? Would this service reduce your labor costs or free up skilled personnel to work more effectively in other areas of your company? Would it help you if I sent a proposal and had one of our account executives phone back in a few days?" In this give-and-take session, which can take less than five minutes of phone time, the skill of the interviewer can generate considerable interest in an offering. How prospects respond to the questions as indicated by vocal tones as well as the content of their answers determines how close a prospect is to becoming a purchaser and thus how the prospect should be rated.

4. RATING LEADS—Leads are traditionally rated as A, B, C, and D or 1, 2, 3 and Dog 4 although these instinctive and subjective ratings provide an oversimplified picture. Managers always need to emphasize that written descriptive records are critical.

    Sample Statements for Class A Leads:

    "Made sale."

    "Prospect said he'll place an initial order for four gross."

    "Wants to know when we can send painters to redecorate the office."

    "Wants to start stocking our product as soon as possible and wants one of our sales people to phone or come by."

When these statements come to a lead finder he or she should be trained to run, not walk, to the manager or the assigned sales representative. This report should not be permitted to gather dust.

Sample Statements For Class B Leads:

"Probable sale."

"Wants to determine whether to make his purchase this month or next. Meantime, would like literature, complete price sheets, and terms."

Such a promising prospect should not be neglected and all responses should be on a tight timetable.

Sample Statements For Class C Leads:

"Wants to discuss with partner."

"Wants to determine if he can afford it."

"Wants to discuss it with her field personnel."

"Would like to buy, but wants to wait a couple of months."

"Wants us to phone in six months."

"Likes present supplier, but might give us a trial after the first of the year."

Although these are not hot prospects, they frequently become important customers. They do not require the tight follow-up of A and B leads, but lead finders should be trained to make commitments for call backs even months down the pike. Every class C lead is a potential class A.

Varying Responses: While all three of the foregoing categories are worth follow-up calls, the calling patterns should vary. The response to an A prospect is obvious. Your staff should treat all calls as a service to the customer. A class B prospect should be pursued at discreet intervals until he or she says "no," or indicates in some other way—perhaps inattentiveness or an unwillingness to come to the phone as reflected in up-tight tones from the receptionist—that there's been a negative change of heart. A class C might be worth only one more call several months from now at which time this prospect either qualifies as a B or becomes a class D.

Class D Leads: If statements made by a prospect as early as the first phone call cannot be converted to C values, the presumed prospect is not a prospect at all and probably never will be. Such an unpromising lead is a costly waste of time and should be abandoned without delay. Typically, the lead finder who cannot undo a set mind using previously effective sales tactics can only report: "No sale. Not interested." Class D "no sales" give any number of stock excuses: Gets all the business desired by word of mouth; too small to afford our product or service; won't do business on the phone. The list of stock responses intended to switch off communications is obviously much longer. Some leads show their hostility by hanging up or showering the lead finder with abuse. One tactic a manager ought to warn his staff about as a matter of cost control is the opposite of "hanging up" in which a class D obviously attempts to engage in a long, meaningless conversation at the caller's expense, feigning interest that is turned on and off like a tap. As a caveat: remember that personnel can move. Calling back in a year might uncover a new person with a new attitude.

THE TEAM APPROACH

Whenever lead generating and sales closing are divided responsibilities, lead finders and closers should be given sales training and booster programs together so that each fully understands the role of the other and is coached to interact effectively.

An effective long-term approach to an operation in which telephone responsibilities are divided is to form teams in which researchers or lead finders feed information to a group manager who then passes it along to the sales team on an equitable basis so that nobody is favored in the quality of the leads. Another effective practice is to team a skilled researcher directly with one or more sales representatives. This permits a smooth transfer of information from the person who gathered it directly to the closers who will use it.

It's always a good idea for a manager to be sure that a lead finder knows as much as possible about how each account executive or closer works. Selling styles vary. Top researchers or lead finders who recognize this and apply it consistently are excellent candidates for group manager posts with responsibility for assigning accounts to sales representatives based on their known strengths.

COMPENSATION FOR LEAD FINDERS

Compensation for telemarketers who do not close sales can be established in a number of ways. The least effective would be an hourly wage or fixed salary with no overrides. Not much better is a productivity rate based entirely on payment per contact. The straight salary provides no incentive to increase sales while payment per contact encourages lead finders to rush through calls and turn in unqualified prospects.

A much better compensation system gives the lead finder a salary guarantee plus a commission on the sales that account executives close. The commission percentage should be based on the unit values of the sale, and in combination with the salary should permit the lead finder to earn roughly 75% of the annual compensation of the account executives being served.

How this might work out is shown in the calculations below.

Average sale = $7,000. Approximately 100 sales/year for this team.

Commission for account executive 10%—$700/sale.

Lead finder's salary = $280 per week.

Average annual earnings of account executive = $70,000.

Lead finder's salary approximately 1/5 account executive's annual income.

For the lead finder to make 75% of the account executive's annual income, or $52,500, the commission must account for $37,940 of annual income. Therefore, the lead finder's share on the sale must come to 5.42% of gross ($379.40), making the total commission cost of the sale 15.42% of the gross.

Of course, there are as many formulas as there are creative managers, but the common denominator running through all the successful ones is that there must be a clear relationship between lead finding and sales closing commissions, and the dollar returns from lead finding must motivate the recipients and elevate the quality of telephone work.

When owners and managers are farsighted enough to reward marketing activities as well as sales, the long-term sales performance of the telemarketing team will be optimized. Quality market research is a sound investment.

KEY POINTS

1. The phone is a powerful sales instrument, but to maximize its potential requires sound marketing.

2. Successful sales people may resist marketing because it is less exciting than selling.

3. An effective telemarketing staff will recognize that a prospect who does not buy can still provide valuable marketing data.

4. Market surveys which do not involve attempted sales are costly and can produce misleading data.

5. The best method for collecting marketing information is a pilot sales program. Such a program yields accurate sales and cost projections and provides suggestions for modifying the product or the sales approach.

6. A division of labor between lead finders and closers can be effective if the two groups are trained to work together closely. Managers need to design a compensation package which will motivate lead finders to carefully qualify prospects.

7. Detailed records which accurately rate leads (A,B,C and D) are essential to optimize the results of marketing research.

CHAPTER 3

THE BASIC CALL: SHOULD IT BE SCRIPTED?

PROS AND CONS

Many telephone sales programs lean heavily on a set script prepared by a sales manager or consultant and placed at eye-level over a purposely narrow telephone desk. Other programs provide callers with one or more fact sheets and train them in improvising responses to prospects' comments.

Scripting may calm upper management's fears since a word-for-word script does not allow much leeway to tarnish the corporate image with ill-considered ad-libs, but we feel it leads to more problems than it solves. Because this judgment puts us at odds with the majority of telemarketers, we will explore the shortcomings of a script-based approach at some length before discussing our preferred alternative.

One apparent value of scripting is that it closely controls a product or service story-line with an exactness that leaves no room for the sales message to become garbled or misunderstood. Much of the fear that a presentation is not going to be effective if a phoner is at liberty to improvise is based on two factors:

1. A fear that telephone technique inherently leads to a higher degree of miscommunication than face-to-face sales confrontations.

2. The perception, which we discussed in Chapter One, that telemarketers are not real sales people.

Each of these reservations has some basis in fact. Communication by phone does lack the element of visual feedback. Without observing facial expressions and body posture, marketers have a harder time discerning nuances of meaning. However, tight scripting tends to increase the miscommunication because the caller is concentrating on getting the words in the script right rather than listening carefully to the prospect.

The perception that telemarketers are not real sales people tends to be a self-fulfilling prophecy. If a company hires unskilled people, treats them as second-class employees, and skimps on their training and compensation, then they will not perform like "real sales people." Scripting will not solve these problems, and it is likely to increase the perception that the company is represented by uncaring, unprofessional robots.

Scripting is sometimes justified as a short-cut for mounting a telephone sales program without requiring callers to be involved in a lengthy training program. Oversimplified statistical standards (number of calls per day) may tempt a manager to sacrifice long-term values for early start-up advantages. When the partition or wall in front of every caller contains a script, a telesales manager can enjoy a sense of security in the knowledge that every prospect is hearing the entire message just as the manager intends. Unfortunately, in most cases the manager's sense of security does not have a good foundation.

What most frequently happens is that a script that attempts to anticipate all the variations in phone dialogue becomes cumbersome and even stultifying. So the script quickly negates itself as a tool because phone representatives begin improvising.

When a set script attempts to place all the right questions in the right places for a phone representative, it generally falls short because beyond the caller's first question, the dialogue has to be tailored to specific needs of the prospect. If a prospect's questions must be answered spontaneously, a script can actually become the string that ties a caller's tongue.

Script hypnosis may also set in when the rote presentation has been given so often a caller no longer listens carefully to the prospect's answers. It's bad form to ask a dentist when he expects to order a .12 inch tap drill. Yet script-hypnosis leads to this kind of error.

Tight scripts give so little play to the imagination and creative responses of high quality sales people that sales may drop simply as a result of boredom.

A SCRIPT FOR DISASTER

There is probably no better example of all the things that can go wrong in scripting than the following case history of a real project that failed for an international corporation in the field of business communications.

The president of the corporate branch and his advisors decided to purchase a bankrupt directory publishing house and retain its owner as a combination manager and computer programmer. The company planned to offer a regional directory for the construction industry and a similar directory for the oil industry. Each directory would have an alphabetical listing of all firms in the region and a Buyers Guide, which would categorize firms by the product or service they offered.

The ex-owner, now directory manager, hired a man he knew socially to be the telemarketing consultant. The consultant came to the program with years of experience selling by phone for various publications.

Hiring and Compensation Mistakes: Scripting became a natural outgrowth of the directory company's ill-conceived hiring and compensation policies. Skilled telemarketers proved hard to find, so to get experienced people the company picked up several "boiler-room" types. Compensation was modest at best, structured as straight commission with advances for slow months. As the project progressed, the forecast sales did not materialize and staff morale plummeted as their monthly draws consistently exceeded commissions, putting everyone in debt. The consultant responded with increased sales pressure, which was soon felt by the prospects as the staff battled for quick closes and paychecks to bail them out of debt. In addition to the script problem, this scenario illustrates several other common mistakes. The company should have hired better and trained better. A better compensation package including a base salary would have lessened the distress of the staff and enabled them to project a relaxed, confident image to prospects. Fortunately, the manager realized his mistake and added a salary component before the project completely collapsed.

The Parrot Script: Against this background, it is not surprising that one of the first acts of the consultant was to write a tight script—a "parrot script"—which he hoped would be followed to the letter by eight sales representatives as they called firms in the construction and oil industries. A "parrot script" is set up so users can accurately repeat the same message in call after call, reading from the copy tacked in front of them.

This script, like so many, attempted too many functions and tried unsuccessfully to anticipate the total dialogue possibilities of every phone call. In the consultant's mind the script would achieve all these functions:

1. To explain the concept of a regional industry directory to prospects who had no previous knowledge of the product.

2. To establish the accuracy of free listings obtained from other data bases.

3. To sell directories at a pre-publication price of $25—a savings of $10 on the post-publication price of $35. If possible, the callers were to obtain multiple purchases from each company contacted.

4. To sell enhanced listings in bold face type with extra wording.

5. To sell display advertising at rates from $40 to $500 depending on the size of ad.

The consultant and manager assumed prospects would welcome the phone calls as soon as they realized they were getting free listings in the alphabetical and Buyers Guide sections of the directory.

Both men were expecting easy book sales, especially since buyers could return unwanted units after 10 days examination. They also believed that enhanced listings and display advertising would sell without any great effort or talent on the part of callers.

Copy used in the script came to approximately 700 words without including variations. Callers were to contact 12,000 firms in a four-state area. The length of the script pushed the average phone conversation in the early days of the project to over 15 minutes.

Six weeks after the project began, some of the callers were still following the script to the letter; others had picked salient features they found effective. None were meeting the sales projections of the consultant.

What does a "parrot script" look like in print? Take a peek.

Mr./Mrs. _____, my name is _____and I'm with _____ in Denver, Colorado, (on local calls say, here in Denver), and this fall we are publishing a Buyer's Guide and Directory for your industry in Texas, (and include Hobbs, NM and Tucson, AZ, if your prospect is in either of these areas). Information on your company is published in a FREE listing at no charge. I'm calling to make sure that the information for this is complete and accurate. I'll also want to talk with you for a few moments about ordering copies of our Directory and Buyer's Guide and about placing display advertising. First, let's make sure that your listing information is correct and, as I mentioned, there is no charge. . . .

The representative is then instructed to read the listing slowly to the prospect and verify its accuracy and completeness. There were many delays at this stage when suspicious prospects questioned the motives behind the phone call. Contractors in New Mexico were especially hostile to the out-of-state publishing company.

If a sales representative weathered the free listing part of the script, he or she then attempted to take a few minutes to physically describe the book which was a totally unknown product in the market being penetrated. Some 100 plus words later, during which everything from format size to indexing and tab features were described, the sales person was again required to remind the prospect of how many free listings the firm would get.

Sinking in the Script: For the first month, some of the most experienced callers on the staff were frequently unable to get past the first paragraph. Prospects were baffled by the free listings. "What do you mean we get a freebie? Nothing is free in this world. Why are you calling me."

One phoner took the floor at a bi-weekly sales meetings to say: "I modified the opening of my script and it worked a little better." In the modified script after the caller identified herself, she said: "I know you don't know me, and I barely know you, but I know something about you because my company has your company on our computer data base which we're using in a directory in your industry. I'd like to verify your listing and get to know you better."

She reported that she did not use the word "free," unless asked until she had the listing verified and was ready to discuss a book sale and/or enhanced listings and advertising sales. What made that change effective was that it snared the prospect's curiosity ("I know something about you.") and invited a relationship ("I'd like to get to know you better.")

That member of the staff would have made a good script writer, but even the best script from somebody else never seems as good as what a strong sales person, who is comfortable in phone sales work, can generate from his or her own nimble mind. Even if this script were changed to incorporate the improved opening, it would break down. "I'd like to get to know you better" invites a comment, and comments from a prospect are the bane of script writers because no one can predict what the prospect will say.

This staffer was intuitively moving toward the non-script approach, which relies on relationship selling, on getting the prospect to talk about his or her concerns and needs. Once the prospect discloses a real need, it is relatively easy to show how our product can meet that need.

The other obvious advantage of the improved opening is its use of the staffer's own words. No one likes to talk to a machine; by speaking in her own natural diction, the caller was able to dispel the lingering distrust we all feel talking to a stranger. Good script writers, of course, try to write natural sounding dialogue, but different callers speak differently. Scripts end up being compromises, full of neutral expressions—sort of like (boring) committee reports.

Aside from some obvious disadvantages in relationship building, when a tight script is prescribed by management, "parroting" breeds boredom for bright men and women who use it day-in and day-out; at worst it can lead to early burnout for the ones who find they can't use the script effectively but who nonetheless become trapped with it as an objective in itself. In less severe cases scripts can dampen the initiative which is critical to sales.

So much for an insight into one script that created more problems than it solved. If you want more exposure to the perils of scripting, simply listen carefully to the sales calls which come to your office and home.

THE INTERACTIVE ALTERNATIVE

If scripts work poorly, what works well?

Laying the Groundwork: A solid telemarketing campaign starts with a strong professional recruiting program in which phone representatives have been selected because they possess exceptional communication skills—including writing skills if follow-up letters will be used.

The second step is an extensive training program in which callers learn about product features and benefits and practice interactive calling.

Developing Fact Sheets: Instead of a script, the marketing director should prepare a poop-sheet that gives all the features of the product with emphasis on the advantages of this product or company compared to the competition. This fact sheet will be a source of key information to be used in the opening of a marketing and sales phone call. It will have a choice of key facts which can be explained in thirty seconds or less to capture a prospect's interest.

Some teams use a second sheet with specific benefits to customers along with key phrases which may be useful with certain types of prospects and key questions to get prospects talking about their needs. Since benefits are in the eye of the beholder, good ideas for this sheet can occur in brainstorming sessions. As with the features sheet, the emphasis should be on ideas which can be conveyed in thirty seconds or less.

With these sheets in hand, a fully trained caller can explore the prospect's needs and select features and benefits which address those needs. With this approach, callers have the freedom to carry on a relaxed natural conversation, and prospects correctly perceive that the company cares about solving their problems and concerns.

Training: Smart managers don't just pass these sheets out. They conduct several training sessions to make sure callers know how to use the tools. In the first session the telemarketing team should review any catalogs, brochures, annual reports, service manuals, or other company literature out of which they can draw background information and useful ideas for their sales presentations. They should also review competitors' material, so they know exactly where their competitive advantages lie.

The team should discuss alternate approaches to prospects, typical objections, likely questions, and other variations that are likely to occur. The last and most important phase of training is to practice simulated phone calls. Maximum simulation in a classroom setting can be achieved by plugging in phones to the public address system. If that is not possible, the caller and the prospect should be seated so they can hear but not see each other (back to back, for instance). Every caller should be exposed to a variety of calling situations: one prospect might be inattentive, another worried about cash flow, some would pick up on one particular feature, others would like something different.

Seeing another person struggle through the variations is not enough; only if a caller does it herself will she have the confidence to handle the situations well when they actually occur. This type of training can be supplemented by periodic monitoring in which a marketing director listens silently to several actual calls and discusses possible improvements with the caller. This type of coaching needs to be upbeat and positive; otherwise, the manager may undermine the caller's confidence and jeopardize his or her effectiveness.

Job candidates should be told early they will be monitored and coached. If the manager advises everyone of this requirement, thin-skinned candidates can withdraw early.

Sample Features Sheet: If the directory campaign had been organized in this manner, the features sheet could have included these facts:

1. The Directory section contains the name, address, phone numbers, locations, affiliations, and key personnel of each company.

2. Alphabetized for easy reference.

3. Covers every company in the industry within a particular region.

4. Buyer's Guide section lists product and service categories. Within each category, companies are listed by cities.

5. Twenty times as many listing categories as the yellow pages.

6. Tabbed for easy reference.

7. Bold-face listings available for a small fee.

8. Display Advertisements available.

9. Advertisers may submit camera-ready copy. Otherwise, proofs will be sent for final approval.

10. Post-publication price of a book will be $35. Pre-publication price is $25. Bulk discounts available.

Sample Benefits Sheet: Another easy-reference sheet could have displayed these benefits:

1. The Buyers Guide with its listing of all product and service categories for the industry makes it easy for you to find a

number of companies that satisfy your requirements. It is an excellent resource for inviting bids.

2. The directory is sold exclusively within the industry, so advertising is closely targeted.

3. It is more complete than trade association directories and gives easier access to listings.

4. Merged/purged listings are more complete and ads are less costly than yellow page advertising.

5. Listings are free of charge.

6. Many more classifications are covered within the industry in the Buyers Guide section than can be covered in the yellow pages.

7. Display ads are highly visible and when executed professionally will build or reinforce your company's image and lead to increased sales.

8. You will find the book handy for desk top, desk drawer, and vehicle glove compartment use.

9. The pre-publication price saves $10.

10. Bulk order prices make it easy to keep a copy at each of your operating locations.

11. If you purchase display advertising, you will get a free copy of the directory.

12. You may return the book within the 10-day free trial period and owe nothing.

Sample Questions: This page or another could also have included sample openings and closings as well as questions to draw out the prospect's needs:

1. You don't know me, but I already know a little about you through our industry directory. I was hoping we could get better acquainted.

2. Have you ever been frustrated at needing to find an industry source when you did not have a good reference?

3. Do you ever wish you could find a cheap source of advertising to reach industry members who don't belong to the association?

4. What kind of buyers would you like to reach within the industry?

5. What types of suppliers do you typically work with? How do you find them?

6. Do you ever feel frustrated trying to find suppliers in the yellow pages?

7. How much time would you save if you could have an industry reference at your elbow?

8. Does this book sound like something you could readily use?

9. Would your other operating locations also benefit from having such a handy reference?

10. Since you can return the book at no cost, are you ready to try one out to see how it can help?

THE COMPLETE DISASTER

With 22 points to cover, the script form was top-heavy and too elaborate to be effective, and the sales representatives were burdened by this complexity from the outset of the campaign. Fact sheets would have reduced the phone presentation to a manageable discussion. Even though the fact sheets had more information, the callers did not have to wade through everything—they could choose points to match the buyers' needs.

The fact that the script forced callers to spend extra time on each call should not be taken lightly. We don't advocate rushing through calls, but the time spent on each call is a critical factor in projecting the feasibility of a telemarketing project.

Managers in the failed directory program discovered this the hard way. Five weeks after callers began working with the unwieldy script, it became apparent they would not meet the deadline for validating directory information. Plus, high phone bills and salaries, coupled with low sales, were eating up the profit margin.

The program was cut back to updating listings and telling prospects that the company was going to send them a book on approval. The desperate option of sending unsolicited books with a "no obligation" guarantee brought returned directories back by the carload at exceedingly high postal costs.

ALTERNATIVE TO DISASTER

If callers had been taught to improvise from fact sheets the disaster might have been avoided or the damage mitigated.

We would expect the marketing campaign to gradually improve as comments by particular prospects generated additional points for the fact sheets. One prospect might be concerned that the firm be included as both a pipe supplier and an equipment supplier in the Buyers Guide. That would prompt the caller to add an additional benefit for future calls: "To ensure the widest possible coverage, we let you determine the appropriate categories for listing your firm."

Unlike the script approach, adding data to the fact sheets with the interactive approach does not drive up long-distance costs. As callers would be addressing only the primary concerns of each prospect, telephone time would be dramatically reduced. Holding down the time on each call would reduce expenses and make it easier to meet the deadline for validating entries. But the most valuable effect would be speeding up the feedback on the program's effectiveness.

If impromptu discussions based on the fact sheets were effective in selling books, but the deadline for validating entries was still in danger, the smart response would be to continue what was working but hire more staff. If the books were not selling, the well-trained callers would be bringing in information on what was going wrong—information management could use to make mid-course corrections.

If prospects felt price was a problem, the price could be changed. If ads were not selling, each buyer of two copies of the book could be offered one small free ad. If most of the book's buyers were concentrated in one segment of the industry, management could cut losses by concentrating selling efforts in that segment while merely validating entries with firms in other categories. None of these actions will magically reverse a difficult situation, but all of them increase the odds of surviving. Also, none of them would be possible without getting prospects to talk and callers to listen and relay critical information to management. At this point it should be obvious a script allows too little two-way interaction for meaningful feedback.

In the worst possible case, if no one was buying books or ads and no corrective action was possible, management would at least know why and could avoid compounding the disaster by sending thousands of books that were certain to be returned C.O.D.

GUIDELINES FOR THE
INTERACTIVE APPROACH

When telemarketers are permitted to develop their own presentations from raw facts, they can be highly effective if they stick to a few rules:

1. Keep it simple.

2. Focus on the customer's interests.

3. Concentrate on benefits that reveal features. Example: "The number of Buyer's Guide listings in our directory gives you many opportunities to cut costs by finding competitive bidders."

4. Be natural.

5. Leave the customer feeling in control. (Don't try to make decisions for a customer.)

A SUCCESSFUL ILLUSTRATION

How would an effective interactive approach sound? Listen to this composite example based on actual experiences:

With the Receptionist:

> "Good morning. I'd like to speak with George Doaks if he's available."

> "Can I tell him who's calling?"

> "Yes, of course. I'm Jan Anderson, calling from Denver.

> "May I ask what company you're with?"

> "Why sure. I'm with Sweet Caress Candy Corporation."

> "May I ask what this is about?"

Since Anderson knows the name of the prospect and suspects the receptionist may be screening calls, a cautious response is best.

> "It will be best if I discuss it with Mr. Doaks."

So far the caller has given the receptionist no reason to screen the call. In all probability if Doaks is available and willing to talk he will be on the line shortly.

The conversation proceeds:

With the Prospect:

> "Doaks here."

> "Hello, Mr. Doaks. I'm Jan Anderson from Denver, and I'm with Sweet Caress Candy."

Callers often have trouble deciding whether to call a new prospect by the first or last name. On this point the two authors part company. Walter belongs to the old school which believes business should be conducted by last names until the client invites us to use a first name. Ray's advice is to notice how people refer to themselves. If the above prospect had answered the phone, "This is Joe Doaks," Ray would have responded, "Hello, Joe." In no case should the caller alter the name: if a person answers the phone as "Steven" or "Janice," don't shorten it to "Steve" or "Jan."

Back to the call:

"Could you call me back? I'm in a conference."

"Of course, when would be a good time?"

"Let's see, can you call about 9:30 tomorrow morning?"

Smart marketing directors train their personnel to keep all callback appointments as close to the agreed time as possible. An appointment is a appointment whether it is kept by phone or in person. Nor does it matter whether the appointment is made for the same day, the following day, a week later, or six months later. Punctuality is still essential.

At first glance, it may seem easier to let Doaks make the return call, but this is not the case. If the telemarketer calls back, he or she can review the fact sheets, "psych up" mentally, and make the usual well-planned sales call. If Doaks calls back, the telemarketer is frequently interrupted or caught off guard. (Is Doaks a prospect for the praline promotion or one of those people we called about late receivables?) As a result the telemarketer comes across as awkward and uncertain—not good traits for completing a sale.

If the prospect must make the return call, set a time when no outgoing calls are planned.

If Doaks doesn't ask for a call at another time, the conversation proceeds into the 30-second zone.

"The reason I'm touching base with some of the candy wholesalers in your area is that Sweet Caress is introducing Praline Puffs, a new type of whipped praline, and to introduce it we are coming out with a limited time offer of three cases for the price of two at the usual 40% wholesaler discount. So that's a double discount. Can I answer some questions for you, or can I ask a few myself?"

The Role of Questions: If the prospect takes the initiative and asks questions that could develop into decision making, the caller has a valid indication of interest with a prospect whose importance is certainly no lower then a B classification. As the caller answers the questions the stage can be set to close the sale and take an order.

Whenever the caller has to ask the questions, he or she should attempt to communicate product values and nudge the prospect toward a favorable decision. Managers should teach the difference between questions that can be answered "yes" or "no", and the heavyweight thought-provokers that are used as tools in either convincing the prospect to buy or discovering what unknown factors may be causing resistance.

The Reluctant Prospect: Questions that turn up usable information focus on why a prospect is reacting negatively and what kinds of purchasing experiences or economic setbacks are influencing the present discussion.

One of the clearest indications that a prospect is wavering is a repetition of questions previously answered. This behavior indicates a need for reassurance that a decision to buy is correct. Unless the telemarketer can find out what is behind the uneasiness, the sale is likely to be lost.

Here are some of the questions that might keep a sale open for Praline Puffs:

1. When was the last time your company introduced a new confection?

2. What special promotion did the manufacturer offer wholesale outlets to boost sales during the introductory period?

3. Was there a strong advertising program?

4. What was the projected sale quantity at the time you received that product?

5. How close were you able to come to meeting projections?

6. What are the factors you like to see in a new candy promotion?

Each of these questions should permit comparisons of strong points in the Sweet Caress operation with a previous marketing program.

The answers to these questions allow for a dialogue in which the caller develops fairly accurate insights into the reasons for the potential purchaser's reactions. When the questioning is professional, the caller builds a relationship and comes to understand the prospect's thinking. Answers to complex questions requiring more than a yes or no response serve as springboards for encouraging prospects to come closer to purchasing decisions by getting them to articulate their needs and think through solutions to those needs.

Consider this sample of how information from a prospect can be woven into an effective sales dialogue. In answer to one of the questions, the prospect states:

> "We introduced this new candy bar eight months ago. They projected first month sales of $100,000. We actually sold $75,000 worth after stocking the full recommended amount on our first order. We weren't too happy with the results."

Support Mailings: If the prospect hadn't mentioned being unhappy with the results, the caller should have asked, "How did you feel about it?" Because Sweet Caress planned its campaign with the errors of its competitor in mind, the caller should be able to offer an effective support statement:

> "In every market we tested with Praline Puffs, we exceeded projections by three percent or more. We had a top market research firm working with us. Would you be interested in seeing the data on which we base projections for your area? We could also send reports on our test marketing."

Whether the answer is "yes" or "no" the ability of the caller to offer supporting literature by mail eliminates the need to fill a script with lengthy background material. In this case a follow-up mailing and further telephone appointments are likely to produce a sale.

Deferred Sales: Not all sales occur on the first phone call. New telemarketers may find it difficult to recognize that some sales can take a year or more. A prospect may have a long buying cycle, or a short-term cash-flow problem, or may simply be so swamped with other issues that a decision needs to be put off. For deferred sales to develop through telephone marketing several things need to occur:

1. The initial phone conversation must be interesting and connect with a real need of the prospect.

2. The backup mailing must support the phone conversation by including the same themes and key expressions.

3. Some part of the mailing must be suitable as a long-term reference.

4. The relationship must be continued through repeated contacts.

To hold the interest of a prospect over a protracted period, a telemarketer has to continue calling at intervals, primarily to ask again if the prospect is ready to buy and to update him or her on any changes in product, service, terms, prices, or policies.

Callers should always be alert to make notes on personal information shared by clients. This information is always valuable, but especially so when working toward a deferred sale. Since the follow-up calls are primarily for maintaining the relationship, friendly conversation becomes a key element. Many a deferred sale has been won by the judicious use of comments like these:

"Have you seen the Bengals play yet?" (To a Cincinnati football fan.)

"How's your daughter doing at Texas Tech?"

"I'll bet you are having fun with that new grandchild!"

A caller engaged in a long-term follow-up effort can be regarded either as a pest or as an excellent calendar secretary for the prospect. Managers should make sure everyone knows the difference. Follow-up calls are welcome if both parties have agreed on when they should be made. Callers can encourage such agreements by fairly simple questions:

> "Would you like me to call you back after you have the budget figures?"

> "When would be a good date to check back?"

> "I can see you have your hands full. Would it be helpful for me to call back the middle of June?"

If a caller makes a further appointment as a matter of courtesy during each follow-up call, the relationship with most prospects can be maintained over surprisingly long periods. But not indefinitely—the series should end when the prospect makes it clear that further phone calls are no longer desirable or it becomes apparent the prospect is no longer in the B or C category.

Callers can easily get involved in friendly long-term relationships that offer only scanty opportunities for a sale. For this reason, it is imperative for managers to audit phones at intervals to ensure low category prospects are being dropped.

Tight scheduling of follow-up calls can be abandoned whenever a telephone representative has new information about a product or a service. Bringing information about important changes to the prospect sooner than the next scheduled follow-up does not impede or break the basic system. If new information does not seem important enough to warrant interrupting the schedule, the telemarketer should make a note to ensure the prospect is brought completely up to date during the next scheduled call.

THE ELEMENTS
OF SUCCESS

The elements of success in interactive telemarketing are relatively simple:

1. Plan well.

2. Hire well.

3. Train well.

4. Support well.

A high-quality telemarketing staff will function much better when given the freedom to improvise and interact with prospects. With this approach an organization can develop long-term profitable relationships.

KEY POINTS

1. A word-for-word phone script, while apparently attractive, can actually be so cumbersome that it stifles motivation and creativity.

2. An interactive approach supported by fact sheets allows telemarketers to concentrate on the prospect's real needs.

3. An interactive approach will be consistently more effective than a script approach in gathering critical marketing information and in establishing long-term profitable relationships.

4. The interactive approach requires that managers hire articulate, confident people and train them well.

5. Interactive telemarketers need to have a thorough understanding of the features and benefits of the project and must be given practice in fielding a variety of questions and comments.

6. Telemarketers must be able to use open-ended questions to draw out the reservations of reluctant prospects.

7. Mutually agreed-on call-backs are the key to deferred sales.

CHAPTER 4

THE DIRECT MAIL CONNECTION

REINFORCING THE SPOKEN WORD

Although it is much cheaper, personal contact by phone closely parallels face-to-face personal contact. An outside sales representative who calls in person will typically leave supporting material with a client or prospect—perhaps a sample, a brochure, or a spec sheet. This material is important since it reinforces the prospect's impression of product values and serves as an ongoing reference.

In a telemarketing campaign the use of direct mail can perform the same function. A judicious combination of telephone calls and mailings can have a synergistic effect as each medium covers the weakness of the other. A smart manager will design a campaign which exploits both the impact of personal phone calls and the staying power of the printed word.

Drawbacks of the Phone-Alone Approach: The need for staying power is illustrated by this scenario. The caller reaches a prospect who is interested but not ready to make a purchasing decision. The caller makes a call-back appointment for two months later. During that 60 days something happens to change the prospect from B to A status. Perhaps the product is an accounting package and the prospect suffers through an IRS audit and realizes how inadequate the present accounting system is. Perhaps the product is business liability insurance and someone falls down the front steps causing the owner to visualize a million-dollar lawsuit. Perhaps the product is a home security system and one of the prospect's neighbors is burglarized. Or, perhaps the reason is mundane—an increase in the budget or a decrease in the workload, which allows time to study the purchasing decision.

In any event, the initial phone call is now a fuzzy memory. The prospect can't remember the features of the product or even the name of the caller. If a competitor reaches the prospect before the sixty-day call-back, the competitor will probably get the sale.

Without direct mail support, some deferred sales will inevitably be lost. Programs that just touch the surface are only effective when a broad market is being attacked with fairly simple products and services. A one-phone-call approach would be reasonable when selling holiday cookies to consumers. The product is easy to understand and does not cost much. Most people would decide during the initial call. Because the product is inexpensive, it has to sell on the first call or the marketing expenses will erase the profit margin. More complex products introduce the need for staying power—to ensure deferred sales are not lost.

Gaining Wide Exposure: Direct mail can reach a mass market much faster than telemarketing. In the second half of this chapter we will discuss how to capitalize on this advantage through a "Mail-First Approach." Before looking at mass markets, though, we need to examine the narrower "Phone-First Approach."

THE PHONE-FIRST APPROACH

In a narrow market where telemarketers have the time to make all the initial contacts, it makes sense to call each prospect before mailing anything. That first phone call greatly reduces the amount of direct mail which ends up in the trash can. Even though the phone call comes first, the follow-up mailing is still important.

However, realizing the need to use the mail as well as the phone does not guarantee the two media will be mutually supportive. To gain this synergistic effect, the marketing staff needs to plan the phone calls, letters, and supporting documents as part of a single package. A staff which fails to achieve that close connection will consistently waste resources.

Drawbacks of Uncoordinated Mail: In a poorly coordinated phone-first campaign, the staff makes phone calls and mails literature, but nothing in the tone of the writing connects it with the voice on the phone. Prospects perceive two independent appeals, neither of which has achieved the critical mass necessary to generate a purchasing decision.

The Coordinated Approach: In all successful phone-mail programs, well-written letters play a key role in supporting what was first said on the telephone, in providing additional data about the product, in holding the prospect's interest during a long buying cycle, in introducing mass-produced printed material (price lists, brochures, catalogs, case histories), and finally in acting as a bridge to future telephone calls and to long-term business relationships.

Achieving close coordination in a phone-mail program is much easier if the person making the phone calls also writes the letters. For that reason, writing skill should be a key factor when selecting new telemarketers. A manager may also want to include letter writing as part of the basic training program. We discuss hiring practices and training programs in more depth in Chapter Ten.

Requirements for a Phone-First Program: Creating a tightly coordinated phone-mail program is not a matter of chance. Success depends on these basic requirements:

1. At the time a program is being designed, the staff needs to select sales themes or product values which will be repeated in the phone calls and the mailings. The fact sheets are built around these common themes and the callers tailor each letter based on the actual phone conversation and the fact sheet data. One way to find effective themes is to call present customers and ask what they like best about the product.

2. All of the follow-up literature and forms should be developed before any caller goes to the phone. Otherwise, sales can be lost because letters cannot be sent until the price sheet or brochure comes back from the printer. Nothing is set in concrete, of course. Marketing data collected in the early phone calls may dictate changes to the telephone approach, the content of letters, or the design of the supporting literature. For that reason you may want to start with short print runs to avoid being stuck with boxes of unusable brochures when the campaign changes.

3. Follow-up letters should have the language traits—vocabulary, key phrases, and sentence structure of the caller's spoken presentation. That repetition is what gives the phone-mail combination more selling power than either the phone or direct mail alone. The value of a sales representative who is persuasive on the phone and can be trained to write cover letters, sales letters, and brochure copy to support the phone calls cannot be overstated. The compensation system needs to reward those people well to keep them on board.

Composing the Follow-up Letter: While each letter reinforces a particular phone call and is tailored to a particular prospect's needs, that does not mean every letter is developed from scratch. A good wordprocessing system makes it fairly easy to modify a sample letter or to pull together fairly standard "boilerplate" paragraphs. If the computer workstations are networked, a caller can pick up good ideas by browsing through co-workers' letters.

To maximize the selling power of follow-up letters, a manager should train the staff to review each letter using this checklist:

1. Does the letter mention the previous phone call? ("I enjoyed talking with you today.")

2. Does the letter repeat key themes in the same words as the phone call?

3. Does the letter or attached material provide additional information?

4. Are all the appropriate attachments or enclosures included? (Consider price lists, catalogs, brochures, advertising reprints, case histories, spec sheets, and testimonials or recommendations.)

5. Is each attachment or enclosure mentioned in the letter, so the reader knows exactly how it fits in?

6. Does the letter contain a bridge to further phone calls? ("I will be checking back after you have a chance to discuss this decision.")

7. Can the letter or supporting material serve as a reference for deferred sales?

8. Is the letter personable? Does it use the words "I," "you," and "we"?

9. Does the letter encourage a long-term relationship?

10. Is the letter one page or less?

The Praline Puffs Campaign: In Chapter Three we discussed an interactive phone call to introduce Praline Puffs to a typical wholesaler. We can now examine how a follow-up letter can be integrated with the initial call.

Jan Anderson, the caller, had established the following points:

1. Praline Puffs are a new type of whipped praline.

2. Distributors get the traditional 40% discount, and for a limited time they can buy three cases for the price of two.

After making the initial statement, the caller encountered resistance and had to keep the discussion alive by asking questions:

1. When was the last time your company introduced a new confection?

2. What special promotion did the candy manufacturer offer wholesale outlets to boost sales during the introductory period?

3. Was there a strong advertising program?

4. What was the projected sale at the time you received that product?

5. How close were you to meeting the projections?

6. What factors do you like to see in a new candy promotion?

Because the marketing staff developed these questions at the same time as the fact sheets, they spring from Sweet Caress promotional strengths. The company plans to launch a major consumer advertising program in the local media. Thus, the telemarketing staff indirectly calls attention to the competitor's weaker advertising effort. Any question which generates a forceful response (positive or negative) should be dealt with not only on the phone, but also in the follow-up letter.

Integrating the Call and the Letter: To see how the initial call and the follow-up letter complement and reinforce each other, compare the words in this call to a second prospective distributor with the words of the follow-up letter.

PHONE

Hello, Ms. Garcia, I'm Jan Anderson with the Sweet Caress Candy Corporation. I'm touching base with some of the candy distributors in your area to discuss Praline Puffs, a new type of whipped Praline *that is long on flavor and light on calories.* In order to introduce it, we have a limited time offer of *three cases for the price of two with the usual 40% wholesaler discount.*

LETTER

It was good talking with you this morning about our new style of whipped praline *that is long on flavor and light on calories.* As I mentioned, we are limiting your risk with a limited time offer of *three cases for the price of two with the usual 40% wholesaler discount.* In effect, we are selling you the product at 60% off retail!

PHONE

We have timed our promotion so you can cash in on *a well-established consumer market by Thanksgiving.* To stay on that schedule, we need your order with the three-for-two discount *no later than August 15.*

LETTER

As I indicated, we're making this offer *effective until August 15* so you can stock the retail outlets in time for our promotion. We intend to have a *well-established consumer market* in your trade area by the time *Thanksgiving* and Christmas roll around.

This distributor, like the previous one, had been burned by overstocking when a manufacturer introduced a new candy product with inflated sales estimates. She is very leery of making the same mistake again.

PHONE

People in your trade area are still buying good candy and if you can put a new line on store shelves at a 60% discount, you have considerable margin for error. We offer an additional advantage because we *tested Praline Puffs in three markets with demographics similar to yours, and sales consistently ranged between 95% and 110% of projections.* To give you *further protection,* we'll set your order up on a *split delivery.* We will ship the first part of the order now and give you *30 extra days* to take delivery of the second part *without penalty or loss of the three for two discount.* Would these safeguards put you in a position to place an order?

LETTER

I'm aware that you were not entirely happy with the CHOCK OLE' introductory program because sales only came to $75,000 when you were given a forecast of $100,000 for the first month. I know when this happens with any of your suppliers we all lose credibility. We are confident sales of Praline Puffs will be from *95% to 110% of projections based on three test markets with demographics similar to yours.* To let you judge for yourself, I am enclosing the reports from those test markets.

We can offer you *additional protection with a split delivery* on your first order. You can split your case order and delay shipment of the second part up to *30 days without penalty or loss of the three-for-two discount.*

PHONE

[Bridge to the letter] In addition to the reports of our test marketing, I will send you samples of our promotional material with a price list and an order form. I'll phone you after you receive these to see if you have any questions. At that time I'll be able to take your order on the phone in order to expedite delivery.

LETTER

[Bridge to the phone] I trust that when I call back in a few days, you will be able to join the hundreds of distributors around the country who are increasing short-term profits on the Praline Puffs introductory offer while permanently building their market share.

Adding Additional Information: In addition to reinforcing points made on the phone, a follow-up letter can add a few additional points or expand on the conversation. As an illustration, consider this letter to a third prospective distributor. In this case the phone call did not cover all the key points.

SWEET CARESS CANDY, INCORPORATED
4567 S. Chambers Road
Aurora CO 80111
(303) 768-4242

(date)

Mr. Herman Washington
Highland Distributing
Road 25 West
Grand Junction, CO 81501

Dear Mr. Washington:

It was good talking with you this morning when I phoned about our new style whipped praline. I indicated that we're offering some unusual advantages to distributors who introduce this new product. I'm sure our special offer of three cases for the price of two with the usual 40% discount will prove enticing.

We are also offering substantial promotional support as documented in my enclosures. To ensure you benefit from the promotion, we ask that your first order be in by the fifteenth of August. This timing will permit you to have your market well organized with a strong consumer demand for Praline Puffs by the time we launch our Thanksgiving promotion.

You'll recall that I mentioned actual sales in our three test markets were 95% to 110% of our initial projections. We had the independent marketing firm of Rogers and Worthington gather and analyze reports from distributors under a variety of conditions and used that data to design consumer advertising programs to support your sales.

We also had the marketing company question distributors as to what protection they would like from us in the introductory program. As a result, we have come up with a split delivery plan. Here is how it works for you.

We will deliver half of your first order as soon as we receive it. We will hold half of your order for three weeks before phoning you to confirm delivery. At that time, you can elect to delay delivery by 30 days, and to modify your case

(letter continues)

load by up to 50% of the remaining shipment. This gives you an opportunity to make your own market test and projection with plenty of safety, since there will be no penalty or change in the basic terms for modifying the order.

I trust that you will want to join the hundreds of distributors around the country who are increasing short-term profits on the Praline Puffs introductory offer while permanently building their share of candy sales in their trade areas. In addition to reports from our test markets, I'm enclosing our consumer advertising schedule, our wholesale price list and recommended retail prices, and our introductory order contract. I trust that when I call back in a few days we'll be able to work together on your initial inventory.

Sincerely,

Jan Anderson
Regional Representative

Crafting the Letter: Although the telemarketer constructed this letter from boiler-plate paragraphs, it is truly personalized. A different phone call would generate a different letter.

For this system to work, the caller-writers must be able to produce letters which sound natural, contain authoritative information, and address the customer's needs.

Preparing the Writers: A telemarketing manager in the early stages of planning a combined phone/mail campaign should hire people who are good writers. (More on hiring in Chapter Ten.) If you forget this advice, you may find yourself trying to teach grammar or basic composition.

Assuming the staff has the basic skills for writing, the manager can concentrate on training the style and content of successful letters. The three qualities mentioned two paragraphs above should be directly addressed in the training program.

QUALITY	TRAINING ACTION
Sound natural	Stress the need to sound natural, not pompous. Have trainees practice writing letters with "I," "we," and "you."
Contain authoritative information	Ensure every trainee understands the product and its benefits.
Address the customer's needs	Coach trainees to listen carefully to each prospect and ask questions to discover needs.

If a company hires and trains its phone staff intelligently, the individual marketers may be able to develop their own sales tools better than the manager could do it for them. The idea is to give a skilled and experienced telemarketer a fact sheet on the product, along with information on pricing, terms, audience demographics, and any other factors that could influence the sale. Then, let the telemarketer prepare the basic letter and a basic telephone fact sheet to go with it. If the two sound good together and meet all the policy requirements of the marketing department, turn that person loose to use the tools.

Staff members who have the required skill will feel more comfortable and be more productive using tools they have produced themselves.

Letting phone representatives write their own correspondence and create their own sales tools has an ancillary benefit. Because telephone sales work involves a mixture of tedium and tension, people wear down during the day. When a telemarketer can turn away from the phone to write a letter, an important break in job monotony occurs. That freedom can increase self-worth and productivity—the two best preventatives for boredom and burnout.

Ghostwriting: For personnel or policy reasons some companies do not let telephone callers write their own letters. Consider the personnel reasons. A manager may not be able to find people who are equally skilled in phoning and writing. Economics or policy may force a company to use people already on board whatever their writing skills. Given the poor quality of writing education in many schools, it is not uncommon to find people who are talented and articulate on the phone—star performers—who write stilted, awkward, even ungrammatical letters. If the problem is not too serious, an outside trainer may be able to come in with a short program to bring everyone up to speed. If only one or two otherwise capable people are having trouble, the company should consider paying their tuition for writing classes at the local community college. If these remedies do not fit, ghostwriting is an acceptable alternative.

Policy reasons for ghostwriting are harder to fathom. Many companies insist on using outside advertising agencies or professional writers regardless of the skills of the telemarketing staff. The intention is to make sure that the product story line is being maintained uniformly and the correspondence looks polished and professional.

This approach carries a significant danger. If the ad agency or writer is carefully chosen, the resulting letters will always look polished, but may have little connection to the phone calls they are supporting. Using a standard letter which is only slightly personalized, sacrifices one of telemarketing's basic strengths—the ability to adapt to the client's particular needs.

A dogmatic policy preference for ghostwriters may also reveal a problem in corporate values. Some executives retain the "boiler-room" image and regard telemarketers as low-level employees with limited skills. If you, as a manager, encounter an insistence on ghostwriting regardless of the staff's writing skills, you should check the corporate culture. No matter who writes the letters, you will not be able to build a quality telemarketing program without hiring quality people and treating them as important, crucial employees.

If the reasons for it are valid, ghostwriting can be made to work so long as the writer has researched the phone callers, taken notes, picked up the way they are phrasing their offer on the telephone, and carried over their phrases in the method shown earlier in this chapter. Writers and callers should work in teams with the caller providing notes on each call or, where it is legal, a tape recording.

Brochures: Literature that is closely coordinated with a phone presentation enhances the phone call. Literature that was prepared for some other purpose with no consideration for the telephone is awkward and difficult to work around. Granted, some multi-purpose brochures can be used effectively in coordination with phone work, but the key piece of writing should still be a personal cover letter phrased like the phone presentation and keyed to client needs.

Adjusting the Campaign: The power of interactive telemarketing is not only in what is said, but also in what is heard. Successful telemarketing managers will train their teams to recognize valuable information and reward them for recording and forwarding it. An alert telemarketing staff can often garner information which will enhance or radically alter a marketing/sales program. Future phone calls and direct mail pieces could both be affected.

If the staff is well-trained, they will immediately notify the manager whenever they experience possible breakthroughs:

1. Windfalls. Unexpected sales, either earlier than expected, more than expected, or coming from an unexpected quarter. A caller selling fax equipment to businesses may discover some business contacts want to buy a machine for home use.

2. Unforeseen product applications which develop in the field. A solvent for cleaning printing press rollers may also work on plastic upholstery.

3. Clear competitive advantages which were previously unrecognized. A client says, "The best thing about your product is the plastic bag. I'm tired of those paper bags spilling stuff all over the floor."

In an imperfect world, all useful feedback is *not* positive. A good staff will also catch and forward important negative information. Notice the importance of the word "BUT" in these comments:

1. "You have a high-quality product, *but* it doesn't fill an immediate need for our company."

2. "I don't know how to fit this into my inventory, *but* it seems as though it ought to sell."

3. "I see its value, *but* I already have something that fills the need."

When the staff brings in this kind of information, an alert manager will re-evaluate the basic strategy to see if either the telephone fact sheet or the draft letter needs to be changed.

THE MAIL-FIRST APPROACH

Alternatives: So far we have discussed telemarketing as if the process always started with a phone call. Several obvious alternatives exist and may work better in certain cases. The initial customer contact could come through advertising (radio, TV, or print) or through direct mail. The ad or mailing would encourage prospects to respond by writing for information, marking a reader response card, or calling a toll-free number. With this approach, the telemarketing staff fields incoming (or inbound) calls or makes outgoing (outbound) calls to follow up on written inquiries.

The advantage of the phone-first approach is improved response. Unless historical data from your industry indicates otherwise, you should expect one to three percent of the target audience to respond to a direct mailing. Most people throw away unsolicited mailings. Contrast that to the phone-first approach: if a prospect asks for information during the initial phone contact, the telemarketer can be reasonably sure the follow-up mailing will be read or at least recognized during the second call.

The advantage of mail-first or ad-first telemarketing is volume. If a telemarketer functions as an account executive, making fairly involved phone calls, he or she can usually average 40-60 calls in an eight-hour day. By contrast, a telemarketer using a simple pitch to sell a simple product on a one-time basis might average 100 calls a day.

If we posit a mass market campaign aimed at 500,000 prospects, direct mail or media advertising could reach all of those people in a week. To make 500,000 phone calls in a week would require a staff of 1,000 to 2,500 trained callers. We could use a smaller staff and lengthen the campaign, but doing so would lessen the impact and could destroy the timing for a new product introduction. Put simply, when the target audience reaches a certain size, phone-first is no longer feasible.

Economic Factors: The costs of generating a qualified lead or a sale by phone will always be cheaper than generating a lead or sale through face-to-face contact. When comparing phone to direct mail, the case is not so clear cut. Which is the cheaper method will vary depending on the product, the prospect list, and other factors.

A company venturing into unfamiliar territory will have difficulty determining the most cost-effective approach, because they have no historical data. In that situation we recommend a three-step approach:

1. Carefully estimate the cost of each approach, using the suggestions given below.

2. Test the estimates using a pilot program. If the start-up costs are high, consider hiring an outside agency to do the mailing or telemarketing. If the pilot is successful, you can scale-up and move the function in-house.

3. Track the actual costs and success ratios of each approach and revise the estimates.

Cost Estimate Guidelines: The two initial approaches, phone-first and mail/ad-first, will ultimately converge if the goal of a program is to establish a long-term client relationship. They will converge because no matter how the initial contact is made, eventually the relationship will develop into a pattern of repeated phone calls or mutually reinforcing calls and letters.

Therefore, to determine which is cheaper we need only track expenses to the point of the initial sale or convergence.

For a phone-first campaign, calculate the cost per sale excluding overhead. We exclude overhead (phone equipment, furniture, office space, utilities) because it will have to be paid anyway if the goal is a permanent telemarketing relationship with clients. To calculate the cost per sale:

1. Estimate the cost per day for one marketing staff member. Remember to use the total compensation package (salary and benefits) plus added costs such as insurance, employer contribution to Social Security, and occupational privilege taxes.

   EXAMPLE: Annual cost per staff member: $60,000. Total working days per year: 240 (365 minus weekends, holidays, vacation, and sick leave). Cost per day: $250.

2. Estimate how many calls it will take to reach the average decision-maker. Allow for wrong numbers, busy signals, call backs, and redirected calls ("Mrs. Bergstrom handles that.")

   EXAMPLE: 3 calls.

3. Knowing what information is needed from the prospect and what needs to be relayed, estimate the average time on the phone with a decision-maker.

   EXAMPLE: 10 minutes.

4. Using the information from Steps 2 and 3, and allowing for breaks, meetings, and interruptions, estimate how many decision-makers one caller can reach in a day.

   EXAMPLE: 36 decision-makers reached each day.

5. Using information from associates and other industry sources, estimate the number of calls it will take before the average decision-maker decides.

   EXAMPLE: 2 calls for a decision.

6. Divide the number of decision-makers reached in a day (Step 4) by the number of calls before a decision is reached (Step 5). The result is the number of purchasing decisions one caller can achieve in one day.

   EXAMPLE: 18 decisions per day.

7. Estimate the percentage of decision-makers who will decide to make a purchase.

   EXAMPLE: 20% will decide to buy.

8. Multiply the number of decisions per day (Step 6) by the percentage of positive decisions (Step 7). The result is the number of sales per day.

   EXAMPLE: 3.6 sales per day.

9. Divide the cost per day (Step 1) by the sales per day (Step 8) to get the cost per sale (excluding overhead).

   EXAMPLE: Cost per sale = $69.44.

Obviously the calculations become firmer as more data becomes available.

Calculating the estimated cost per sale of the mail/ad-first approach is similar.

1. Estimate the total cost for a mailing or ad. For a mailing, include the contract or labor costs for designing, printing, stuffing, stamping, and mailing, plus the costs of envelopes and postage. Determine the total number of prospects reached.

   EXAMPLE: $6,000 total cost; 10,000 prospects reached.

2. Estimate the response rate based on information from similar campaigns.

   EXAMPLE: 3% response.

3. Multiply the prospects reached (Step 1) by the response percentage (Step 2) to get the number of initial responses.

   EXAMPLE: 300 initial responses, which require follow-up phone calls.

4. Divide the total cost of the ad or mailing (Step 1) by the number of initial responses (Step 3) to get the cost per response.

   EXAMPLE: $20 for each initial response.

5. Estimate the cost per day for one marketing staff member.

   EXAMPLE: Cost per day: $250.

6. Estimate how many calls it will take to reach the average decision-maker.

   EXAMPLE: 2 calls. (Since the caller already knows the name and phone number, the number of calls should be less than in the phone-first approach.)

7. Estimate the average time on the phone with a decision-maker.

   EXAMPLE: 8 minutes. (Less than in the phone-first approach because the decision-maker knows more about the product and the caller has some of the needed information already.)

8. Estimate how many decision-makers one caller can reach in a day.

   EXAMPLE: 54 decision-makers reached each day.

9. Estimate the number of calls it will take before the average decision-maker decides.

EXAMPLE: 2 calls for a decision.

10. Calculate the number of purchasing decisions one caller can achieve in one day.

    EXAMPLE: 27 decisions per day.

11. Estimate the percentage of decision-makers who will decide to make a purchase.

    EXAMPLE: 33% will decide to buy. (This percentage is significantly higher because most of the initial responses were from genuinely interested people.)

12. Calculate the number of sales per day.

    EXAMPLE: 9 sales per day.

13. Divide the telemarketing cost per day (Step 5) by the sales per day (Step 12) to get the telemarketing cost per sale (excluding overhead).

    EXAMPLE: Telemarketing cost per sale = $27.78.

14. Divide the cost per response (Step 4) by the percentage of buyers (Step 11) to get the direct mail/advertisement cost per sale.

    EXAMPLE: Direct mail cost per sale = $60.61.

15. Add the telemarketing cost per sale (Step 13) and the direct mail/advertisement cost per sale (Step 14) to get the total cost per sale.

    EXAMPLE: Total cost per sale = $88.39.

Obviously, if the projected numbers show too high a cost per sale, the manager needs to rethink the concept, even before attempting a pilot project.

The Toll-Free Option: Including a toll-free number in the ad or direct mailing is an attractive option, but one which should be evaluated carefully. Consultants Kathy Masi and Connie Bates believe adding a toll-free 800 number will increase the total initial response between 20 and 40 percent. ("Generating Sales Leads With Telemarketing," *Telemarketing*, July 1990, p. 41.)

To complicate the picture, the toll-free number drives up the cost in a subtle way. Between 40 and 60 percent of the people who would otherwise mark the reader response card or mail a coupon will now call the toll-free number. And because calling the toll-free number is easier, it attracts less serious prospects, lowering the percentage of sales.

Notice how a toll-free number affects the calculations for a mail-first or ad-first campaign.

1. The 300 initial responses increase by 20% to 360; of that number half are in writing and half are via the toll-free number.

2. Each toll-free call costs approximately $6.00 since the calls are fairly involved. With 50% of the total responses (180) by phone, the total phone expense is $1080.

3. The initial advertising or mailing expense was $6,000. Adding the toll-free phone expense to that gives a total of $7,080 needed to generate the initial 360 responses.

4. Dividing $7,080 by 360 shows the average cost for each initial response is now $19.67 instead of $20. Described in incremental terms, the 60 additional responses cost $18 each ($1080 divided by 60).

5. Because some people call the toll-free number on impulse, we should assume the percentage of call-in prospects who ultimately make a purchase is half what it was for written responses; only 16.5% will buy. Dividing the cost of each response ($18) by the percentage of buyers (16.5%) gives a direct mail cost per sale of $109.09 for the 60 incremental responses. The same figure for the original 300 responses was $60.61.

Other reasons may require a toll-free number in advertising or direct mail. ("In this industry everybody does it.") Nevertheless, every telemarketing manager should examine the cost-per-sale figures carefully before jumping on the toll-free bandwagon.

Who Writes the Ads and Letters: Producing effective ads requires not only skill in a unique form of writing, but knowledge of the media in a particular area and familiarity with the available talent and production facilities. Unless an entrepreneur has that skill and knowledge available in-house, we strongly recommend using an ad agency.

Because a mass-produced direct mail letter is broader and less personal than the letter which follows a phone call, there is no particular reason to have the letter written by one of the telephone callers. The writing can be performed by an advertising agency copywriter, an in-house direct mail writer, an outside professional, or the telemarketing manager, provided the letter is closely connected to the themes on the telephone fact sheets.

Increasing the Toll-Free Response: The disappointing cost per sale estimates for a toll-free number can be improved by increasing the response rate. One way to encourage readers of an advertisement or a letter to use a toll-free number is to offer more information and a valuable premium from an executive in the company. Here's the text of a letter which might be sent by the company president to introduce Praline Puffs to 100,000 retailers across the country.

> Our new PRALINE PUFFS can put weight on your year-end profits without fattening your customers.
>
> We designed this new confection to fill a hole in your inventory. Because they are high in taste and low in calories, PRALINE PUFFS appeal to traditional candy lovers who are weight conscious.
>
> This letter is your authorization to use our toll-free 800 number to learn about our limited-time introductory offer. Because we value your business, we will give you a detailed demographic analysis of the candy buyers in your area—just for calling 1-800-446-1943.

At the same time you can find out about our limited-time introductory offer of three cases for the price of two (on top of the usual 40% discount). When you telephone, one of our representatives will be happy to answer any questions. Our recommendations on the effective volume for your introductory order will be based on demographics and candy consumption in your trade area. Our research has been done by the firm of Rogers and Worthington, and in our test markets actual sales have been between 95% and 110% of projections.

Along with your market analysis, we will send a sample of PRALINE PUFFS, so you can see why consumers in our test markets loved them.

We believe you will quickly discover that the PRALINE PUFFS program is unique because we share important market research with you while giving you extra profit opportunities in your most important selling season.

By calling us today, you can have PRALINE PUFFS on your shelves before our Thanksgiving-Christmas promotion begins. To get your free demographic analysis and lay plans for increased holiday profits, call 1-800-446-1943 without delay.

Reducing Cost: To reduce expenses, Sweet Caress Candy could make the same offer, but list an ordinary business line. Since the prospects would be paying for the call, the response would be significantly less, but only serious prospects would call.

If time were not critical, the same type of program could be mounted with a postage-free business reply card followed up by a phone call. Two paragraphs of the letter would read:

By returning the enclosed postage-free card, you can receive a detailed demographic analysis of the candy buyers in your area—a tool that will prove useful whatever candy lines you stock.

After you have a chance to examine the demographic analysis, one of our representatives will call to explain our limited-time introductory offer of three cases for the price of two (on top of the usual 40% discount).

Providing Response Options: A business reply card can also give prospects a choice of alternatives:

1. Telephone me.

2. Send complete information.

3. Please ship.

These options can relieve telephone traffic, save time and money, and spread out the order processing. When circumstances permit, offering options makes the most economic use of direct mail with a response mechanism.

Inbound Calls: Inbound calls are trickier than outbound calls because the staff member who answers does not know initially who is calling and does not have a chance to review information. If a campaign has incoming calls as a major component, the manager must ensure that experienced, well-trained people are standing by when the calls are expected.

Guidelines for inbound calls will vary based on the nature of the company and the objectives and strategy of the marketing campaign. You should start with these guidelines and modify them as necessary.

1. PREPARE TO ANSWER: Before picking up the phone, visually locate the fact sheets, price sheet, and order forms. Pick up a pencil and note pad. Clear the mind of distractions, and smile. Smiles carry over the phone, so some telemarketing managers provide every workstation with a mirror. (Check the smile before picking up.)

2. ANSWER PROMPTLY: By the first ring, if possible. Always by the third ring. Promptness leaves an impression of efficiency.

3. IDENTIFY THE COMPANY: The first person to answer an outside line should give a *short* company greeting. This is not the place for an extended advertisement. One of the authors uses, "Welcome to ComSkills"; the other uses "Good morning (afternoon). This is Walter Woolfson and Company." If calls have to be routed (a bad idea for telemarketing), the second person should not repeat the company greeting but only identify the department.

4. IDENTIFY YOURSELF: The style varies based on who is answering. A receptionist or order-taker would only use a first name, "This is Chris." An account executive would use both names, "This is Chris Balkin." (Remember in a long-term telemarketing relationship, the staff members function like account executives, whatever their titles.) A secretary would also mention the boss, "Gail Pollard's office. This is Lynn."

5. USE THE CALLER'S NAME: Doing so places the call on a friendly basis.

6. DO NOT RUSH OR INTERRUPT THE CALLER: Given enough time, the caller may volunteer all the needed information. Take careful notes. If something is not clear, wait for an opportune time to request clarification.

7. SHIFT TO YOUR AGENDA: In addition to asking questions for information ("How did you hear about us?"), ask questions to shift the discussion to the product's benefits and the prospect's needs. "What advantages could you gain from a low-calorie confection?" "Do potential customers ever say, 'I wish all this stuff weren't so rich'?" Once the call is shifted to your agenda, the conversation follows the same pattern as an outbound call.

Using Pilot Programs: Although mass mailing is low-priced on a per capita basis, the total cost for a large campaign can be immense.

When time is not critical, a pilot program can reduce the risk. We believe a short run on the first print order makes sense no matter how good the materials look. The manager should put together the small pilot program just as he believes the full-scale program should be structured. If it works, scale-up immediately. If glitches occur, they can be dealt with before investing more resources.

Mail-First in Narrow Markets: As potent as the phone/mail/ phone integration is in narrow markets, there are at least ten circumstances besides mass marketing requirements when a lead letter is likely to be more effective than the phone-first approach. Here they are:

1. Research and development of a new product that's not quite ready for broad marketing dictates a pilot mass mailing. This approach can garner valuable information, especially if the mailing is followed by phone calls to find out exactly why people responded in certain ways.

2. Both the company and the product are unknown in the target market. Because the market is narrow, intensive interactive telemarketing is the best long-term approach, but you need some name recognition first.

3. So many competitors are selling by phone that a hostile market has developed, resulting in poor sales ratios when the first contact is by phone.

4. The offer is complex. In attempting to get all the information across on the phone, callers either bore the prospects or come across as scam artists.

5. It is important to have the means of concluding the transaction in the hands of the prospect and well understood before the telephone sale is undertaken.

6. Risk factors in the offer must be fully defined and disclosed in order to meet SEC or other regulations.

7. Finding and compensating a high-quality telephone staff is so difficult that management decides to use a group that is much

smaller than the statistics of the program require. Therefore the telephone staff concentrates on the best leads and mail is used to obtain a quick read on the broad base.

8. The staff initially uses the phone with what appears to be an excellent marketing approach and offer, but they encounter a hostile market that refuses to believe them. Monitoring the staff's calls reveals no lapses in professional standards.

9. Some bad phone work by recently fired staff members has created misconceptions about the company that need to cleared up quickly. Mail and public media can help erase misconceptions before new people go to the phone to continue dealing with the problem while restarting the normal marketing process.

10. Management wants to transform a market accustomed to a traveling salesforce into one that is receptive to telephone representatives. A series of letters explaining the benefits of the new approach can smooth the transition before the first wave of phone calls.

Connecting the Letter and the First Call: Each of these ten situations requires a different letter, but every one of the letters should be designed to lead into a phone conversation since the telephone is the key to a long-term relationship.

The following letter is intended to pave the way for telephone sales in a market where competitors are on the phone constantly and many of the targets feel they are being bombarded with unwanted calls (Situation 3 above). Notice how the letter carefully establishes the ensuing phone call.

You don't know me, and I don't know you yet, and if I were to telephone you instead of sending this letter, you'd probably hang up because you're getting so many calls from stockbrokers these days. I wouldn't blame you for your reaction.

The problem for both of us is that you're bound to miss some investment opportunities you might like to consider if only the investment companies would give you a chance to think. I have some stock issues I'd like you to think about, and If we can find a time that will be convenient for you, I'm sure you won't regret our phone conversation.

As we both know, a phone discussion won't obligate you to do business with me. On the other hand, even if you already have an excellent program with another broker, you might still want to consider some of the investments I favor, and might want me on your investment counseling team to manage the ones I know best. In investment planning, it's sometimes better to have more than one company helping to build your portfolio.

Frequently the services of investment counselors from two different firms help create stronger investment mixes than a single stockbroker working alone can provide.

We can discuss these matters if you'll just mark the appropriate boxes on the enclosed postage-free response card and return it to me. The few seconds you take writing in the times and days of the week that suit you best will be well spent.

I'll adhere to your schedule closely when I make a telephone call to set a specific time for our phone discussion, and I'll make the discussion one of the most productive and comfortable ones you've ever had with a broker, either by phone or face-to-face. Won't you mail your card today? Or if you want to open our discussion immediately, just phone me at 265-7794. I'm sure we can turn the telephone into an excellent investment research tool on a streamlined timetable.

The Handwritten Approach: Many managers and executives feel inundated by the daily flood of paper pouring into their in-baskets.

That sensation is the principal reason a phone call prior to a letter will dramatically increase the response rate of the letter.

However, as we have seen from the previous example, phone calls can also be rejected out of hand. One technique to break through both logjams is a handwritten note. A handwritten note in a pile of unsolicited correspondence arouses curiosity. A typical manager will shove aside what looks like bulk mail and open the note first.

For the note to work, it must have a very simple objective. All we want to do is open the door for the phone call. To accomplish that, the note should have these characteristics:

1. Write on simple, but classy, stationery, either white or ivory in color. Try to use monarch size, which is smaller than a business letter, but larger than typical stationery.

2. Write both the envelope and note in blue ink, preferably blue ink which resembles the lines from a fountain pen.

3. Do *not* put a return address on the envelope, but do put one at the bottom of the note (where it may be machine printed). Do not use a logo.

The text should be composed by the person who will make the subsequent phone call. The following model works well because it is polite and to the point.

(date)

Dear Mr. Hopkins:

Because I know a man in your position has a chronically tight schedule, I don't want to interrupt with an unwanted phone call.

I would like to acquaint you with an unusually effective security service not offered by any other company. With your concurrence I will make an appointment with your secretary to phone at a time when you will be free for ten minutes.

(letter continues)

Should you prefer not to be called, have your secretary notify me at 681-3832.

Sincerely,

Pat Bykowski

This approach is relatively time-consuming, thus expensive, but when used correctly it significantly increases the acceptance rate of the first phone call.

The approach works, not only because the note stands out in a sea of typewritten and computer-printed mail, but because it conveys personal concern. The writer is willing to take time with individual prospects because the note is hand-written. The writer respects the reader's packed schedule and would rather lose a contact than create an inconvenience. In short, the writer is a person who is easy to work with and attuned to the client's needs.

A note like this should always be composed by the person who will make the phone call, but handwriting problems or time constraints may require it to be penned by another hand. Since subsequent correspondence will be typed, the reader will never find out the original note was "ghost-penned." However, the scribe should be the same sex as the caller since some people can tell the difference between a man's handwriting and a woman's. Also, the signature of the caller should not be radically different from the rest of the note.

Clean Mailing Lists: Integrating the telephone with direct mail won't work without a strong, clean mailing list in the market you're attempting to penetrate. A good list will have not only the name and address of the company, but the telephone numbers and the names of decision-makers who need your product. Having the right name eliminates a string of frustrating ("I'm not sure who handles that") phone calls.

A list which is incomplete or out-of-date is nearly useless and very expensive to refine. Time-consuming research by your telemarketing staff to develop a list that you're not going to sell to other companies is likely to be uneconomical.

For example, if you were given only companies and phone numbers in a telemarketing list, you would need to have your phone crew contact each company on the list to obtain addresses, zip codes, and information on whom to phone and write before you could do a mailing. On the other side of this coin, a perfect list lacking telephone numbers would require you to have your personnel consult the telephone books and other industrial/commercial directories before anyone could make a call.

Compiling a Mailing List: Although refining an outside list is costly, developing an inside list using the company staff can pay off handsomely despite the time involved. This paradox is true because the best possible list for a new product is a list of people who have purchased one of the company's other products. The second most desirable list is composed of people who have not purchased but did indicate an interest.

Several simple techniques work well in compiling a high-quality inside list:

1. Poll everyone in the company asking them to share their personal contacts.

2. Advertise in the industry media, offering a free newsletter subscription to anyone who will send in a name, address, and phone.

3. Have someone compile a list from old sales receipts (especially useful for retail sales, where accounts are not usually tracked).

4. Have a grand opening or a trade show booth with a drawing for the product you will be selling or a related product. Cards for the drawing are not valid without a name, address, and phone. Drawing for a related product ensures a high-quality list. People with no interest in your product line won't enter.

Buying Mailing Lists: A manager who wants a high-quality, targeted list can either purchase one from the source or go to a mailing list vendor. As an example, if the target was businesses in a given community, one good source would be the Chamber of Commerce mailing list.

Similarly, an entrepreneur who makes and sells auxiliary gas tanks and toolboxes for trucks could trade customer lists with a seller of pickup campers.

Lists are available in various formats, but the easiest to use is pressure sensitive labels for the mailing, accompanied by a a second set of labels with the same names and addresses, but with the phone numbers added. The labels with phone numbers will serve as a reference for entering data in the computer. After that process, each label can be stuck on a file folder or data record, thus providing an organized record-keeping system for the telephone phase.

The best professional list companies guarantee a high level of mail delivery, refunding costs of both lists and postage on returned mail exceeding a stated percentage. List vendors use the information from returns to clean up their lists on an continuing basis. So the refund program is a sign the supplier can be trusted for product quality.

When working with a list supplier, investigate various ways of refining or structuring the list. If you are selling a product which is linked to a certain lifestyle (cellular car phones), ask if the list can be limited to people above a certain income level. If income data is not directly available, the same purpose could be accomplished by screening out addresses in lower-priced neighborhoods. Limiting the list will make it cheaper, save postage and printing costs, and also save time for the telephone team.

Lists can also be sorted in various ways. The U.S. Postal Service grants reduced rates when bulk mail is sorted to their standards. Having the computer sort the labels before printing is vastly more efficient than having the mailing crew sort the envelopes.

Pursuing Procrastinators: No list, no matter how refined, will generate a 100% success ratio. As we have seen, the response ratio from a well-designed mailing can be as low as one percent, but a diligent telephone staff can often increase the ratio by contacting those who did not respond.

Consider a company setting up to sell one high-priced product which is difficult to manufacture. Projected plant capacity is 80 to 110 units per year. The only high-quality list available has only 2,500 prospects. Management decides to use a direct mailing to generate a few orders quickly to get production started.

The initial mailing generates 50 responses (2%); phone calls to those 50 garner 15 orders. Now that production is started, management must decide what to do next. If the company is to survive over the long haul it must find more prospects or improve the sales ratio.

Consider the latter approach. What of the 2,450 addressees who received the initial letter and did not respond to it? Were all of them really uninterested? That's not likely. The probability is that most were too busy to fully consider the offer, or if they considered it, too busy to follow through. Every such group has a high percentage of procrastinators. Stirring them to action could be the most cost-effective avenue to more business.

The telemarketing group can effectively forget the first letter and revert to a simple phone/mail/phone sequence with as few as two or three callers assigned to this follow-up.

Two callers, making as few as 50 phone calls a day and reaching only 20 decision-makers, can conduct at least 200 significant marketing transactions in a normal work week. At that rate the complete list can be contacted in a 12 week period. For each phone staffer added to the first two, the total time for the project can be reduced by a direct ratio, so that a staff of four would take only six weeks to cover the list and a staff of six would take four weeks.

If the mailing was well designed, enough non-respondents would identify the phone call with the mailing to justify the mailing costs even if there had been zero response by mail. Phone representatives, calling into a somewhat softened market, could expect to have higher response ratios than if the initial letter had never been sent.

Even so, the program should be constructed to include a follow-up letter after the first phone call, possibly including the literature sent in the initial mailing. Remember, brochures and spec sheets have staying power.

When strong mailings are teamed in any logical sequence with strong telephone campaigns, the combination becomes as effective as a traveling sales force, but at a fraction of the cost.

KEY POINTS

1. Telephone calls and direct mail can be combined in a mutually reinforcing program. This approach is frequently more effective than either phone calls or direct mail alone.

2. Phone calls are more flexible than direct mail and generate more responses. By contrast, mail offers staying power: the prospect has written material to refer to between phone calls.

3. In a successful phone-mail campaign the follow-up letters and forms will repeat themes and wording from the phone calls. Each letter and phone call will prepare the prospect for the next contact.

4. Because follow-up letters mirror the preceding phone calls, the letters should be written by the people who make the calls.

5. In a mass market, the phone-first approach will be too slow. To get faster results, send a mass mailing and follow up with a phone call to everyone who responds.

6. Having a toll-free number for prospects to call will increase responses, but at a higher cost. Calculate the estimated cost per sale before jumping on the toll-free bandwagon.

7. To increase toll-free response rates, offer free information or a valuable premium to respondents.

8. Inbound calls are trickier to handle than outbound calls. The manager must have experienced, well-trained people available when incoming calls are expected.

9. Mass mailings are cheap *per capita*, but expensive *in toto*. No matter how good the printed materials look, have a short print run and conduct a pilot program to refine the approach.

10. A brief handwritten note can open the door for a subsequent phone call.

11. Successful direct mail campaigns depend on mailing lists which are up-to-date and contain all necessary information.

12. A good list can be compiled from inside sources or purchased from outside sources. In either case the list should be refined by screening out unlikely prospects.

CHAPTER 5

HOW TO FIT PRODUCTS AND SERVICES TO PHONE SELLING

ALL PRODUCTS ARE NOT CREATED EQUAL

The rapid growth of telemarketing attests to its utility as a sales tool. But it is not equally suited to all applications. Some sales functions are easily done by phone; others are more difficult. Some products move rapidly in a telephone campaign; others clutter the shelves. To succeed at telemarketing requires an ability to find or create those situations which are optimal for a telemarketing approach.

ACCOUNT MANAGEMENT

Much of the recent spectacular growth in telemarketing has come from converting the methods of business-to-business account management, that is replacing traveling account representatives with telemarketing representatives. A manufacturer's representative for a line of hand tools sold in hardware stores today is likely to be doing his job over the phone instead of traveling a circuit as he did ten years ago.

Because of the telephone's obvious advantages to an account manager, other uses for telemarketing tend to be forgotten. Indeed, some books on telemarketing ignore all other uses and concentrate on business-to-business accounts.

While not ignoring the other selling situations, we will discuss account management first because it provides a useful model which can be adapted for other applications.

Old Customers, Old Products: The traditional traveling representative provides several services for established accounts: depending on the product, he will arrange displays, conduct inventories, take orders, deliver stock, perform maintenance and trouble-shooting, and provide an important intangible—personal contact.

Many people engaged in field sales will insist all these functions can be done better face-to-face and most are impossible to do by telephone. If we look at actual situations, however, we find all of the functions but delivery can be done remotely, and delivery can be arranged. In many cases doing the function remotely is an improvement from the customer's standpoint.

Consider one such customer, a local outlet selling electrical components to contractors. Under the old system, a manufacturer's representative visits the customer once a month and performs all the above functions except delivery. The customer rarely uses a point-of-purchase display, so that function has little value. The customer occasionally runs out of certain lines, but can't afford to carry a larger inventory. Theoretically, the customer could order by phone between visits by the manufacturer's representative, but that would require a time-consuming inventory. Another annoyance is the timing of the representative's visits. Frequently the representative shows up at the same time two local contractors are wanting service.

This is typical of an old account with established product lines which would benefit from a switch to telemarketing. Under the new system, the customer's inventory would be updated daily using data collected by the computerized cash register. The frequently inconvenient monthly visit is replaced by weekly phone calls. If the customer can't talk when the call comes in, the account representative makes an appointment for a better time. Should the computerized inventory report show a heavier than usual demand for one product, the account representative will make a special call to alert the customer that a bin may soon be empty. At the time of each call, the representative will provide service information and take orders by fax or phone.

From the customer's standpoint, every aspect of the switch to telemarketing is a plus. The new system is less intrusive and responds quicker to his needs. The increased personal contact leads the customer to perceive the company as friendlier and more service-oriented. From the supplier's standpoint, servicing the account is now considerably cheaper since all the phone calls combined total considerably less time than driving to see the customer.

A company selling cookies to grocery stores will find a different result when analyzing a typical account. Each sales representative of this company drives a panel truck loaded with all the current cookie lines. To maintain its quality image, the company insists on a strict "stales policy." Every package is dated, and outdated packages are removed promptly. The representative visits every store weekly to restock and rearrange the display, remove outdated packages, and discuss future needs with the store manager. Switching this type of account to telemarketing would reduce service and perceived value and would not save much money. Because of the stales policy, someone has to make a delivery every week anyway.

A third case illustrates the importance of economic factors in deciding whether to convert old accounts to telemarketing. A distributor of electric motors and associated fittings for oil field applications has a small but steady account in a remote location. The company has one representative who visits each account location quarterly. Between visits the distributor takes orders and provides service information over the phone. On each visit the rep evaluates the installed equipment and makes recommendations about needed repairs and maintenance, possible upgrades, and future applications. This on-site expertise gives the company a competitive advantage.

Unfortunately, the small, remote account does not generate enough sales to justify continued visits. Telemarketing is not an ideal solution: while the company representative can still give advice, he cannot see or hear the installed equipment. However, the alternatives are worse; calling the customer at appropriate intervals provides a viable alternative to dropping the account or discontinuing all customer service.

Evaluating Alternatives: Any company which currently employs an outside sales force should carefully evaluate that practice and consider alternatives. If most of the sales force is simply traveling a circuit to take orders, a change is definitely needed.

This type of evaluation may encounter resistance and active attempts at sabotage by the outside sales force. Strong resistance may indicate valid objections or it may mean the traveling sales people enjoy their life-style and will guard it against any sign of progress. See Appendix 1 for suggestions on dealing with resistance.

A company selling established products to established accounts needs to evaluate the impact of telemarketing across the board and also on individual accounts.

Many activities once thought to require face-to-face visits can actually be done equally well and faster by phone. An outside sales force is not required for any of these activities:

1. Taking and processing orders.

2. Checking inventory.

3. Arranging delivery schedules.

4. Negotiating prices and terms.

5. Providing background on the company and its services.

6. Collecting information on customer needs.

7. Providing product information.

8. Resolving problems with billing, shipping, or defective merchandise.

9. Setting up displays (consider sending display materials, plus a picture and diagram).

For an established product, a face-to-face visit is necessary only under the following conditions:

1. A question about defects, service, or applications which can only be resolved by an on-site inspection. (Perhaps the defective equipment is permanently installed). This is the situation with the oil field electric company described above.

2. The client needs assistance with public relations. If a civil engineering firm suggests a flexible roof for the new city airport, the roof manufacturer may need to send a representative to the city council meeting.

3. The company needs to remove merchandise during deliveries (as with the cookie company's "stales policy").

4. Something changes at the client company. Perhaps the representative has to deal with a different department or a new person on the job.

Some account managers like to make periodic goodwill visits to cement relationships, to reacquaint themselves with the client's situation, and to look for indications of changing circumstances. This approach can be useful if it is focused on the client and his needs; it should not be just a holiday from the telephone.

New Products: When a new product is introduced, the company representative may need to visit old accounts for other reasons:

1. To demonstrate the product.

2. To train the client's staff.

3. To study the client's situation and recommend specific configurations for equipment (i.e., How large a hard disk does the computer need? Is the cooling pond large enough?).

The first two of these functions may also be done remotely by sending a pre-packaged program. (Consider samples, printed instructions, video, interactive video, and computer-based training.) Even an expensive package may be less costly than sending a person to a number of distant sites.

New Accounts: Telephone sales programs are generally believed to be more difficult and less effective than full contact face-to-face sales methods. This is nothing less than the mythology of tradition. Management groups that can't escape the myth are immediately convinced that sales by phone are not practical because demonstration capabilities are lost when the telephone is used to conduct all elements of selling from openings to closings. But with careful planning a company can often develop an effective substitute for a live demonstration.

Alternatives to Live Demonstrations: Assuming an average cost of $300 for a face-to-face call, we can find less expensive (and often more effective) alternatives. Consider these:

1. A professionally made videotape demonstrating a new product. If an account representative demonstrates an expensive product in person, the product leaves with him, but a videotape stays around so others involved in a major purchase decision can see it. The video can also show customer reactions and shots of the product installed and operating at various locations.

2. Models—something that looks like the product, but isn't. If the product is too large to fit in an office, the model could be smaller. If the product is too small to see, the model could be larger. Models can also come apart to show internal parts. Sending fairly expensive models to serious prospects is still cheaper than making in-person calls at three hundred dollars.

3. Samples—the real thing (a bag of cookies, a new design O-ring, a partial financial analysis). These can also be expensive, but economical compared to an in-person call. Some products can be modified so the prospect can see the benefits but still must buy the product to gain very much. A computer program can be shortened; a company-wide leadership inventory can be limited to one person; a research service can be offered free for one week only.

A carefully planned, well integrated campaign will precede these remote demonstrations with introductory phone calls, will send the demonstration kits only to serious, qualified prospects, and will follow-up with phone calls to conclude the sales.

MAKING THE UNSEEN VIVID

When telemarketing supplants a traveling sales force, an interesting phenomenon occurs. Old management theories about tangible and intangible products start to crumble. On the telephone, even a diamond, which is the world's hardest natural substance and which always must be judged by specific physical properties, becomes an intangible. It loses its tangibility by its remote location from the prospect, and it must be made tangible again both by the verbal description and by an enlargement of a microscopic photograph that reveals the identifying patterns and flaws that can be scientifically evaluated by a trained gemologist.

Other intangible products and services by old fashioned definitions can be made tangible by techniques similar to the one used to restore a diamond's tangibility—specific descriptions on the phone, followed by written descriptions and specific illustrations in the mail.

CONSUMER ACCOUNT MANAGEMENT

As more business-to-business accounts are converted to telemarketing, consumer products are also being re-examined. If a product is suitable for an account management approach, the company which converts early can have a significant advantage.

To see how consumer account management might work, consider the traditional operating methods of stockbrokers and other securities dealers. An account representative at a brokerage house will call an investor client at periodic intervals to explain new opportunities or suggest changes in the client's portfolio.

The same approach can work for other consumer products, but not all of them. Account management is a viable approach to consumers if the product is needed on a recurring basis and the profit margin is relatively high. A product like typing paper would not qualify because even a well-to-do family would not use enough to justify the phone calls. Washing machines would not qualify because they need only infrequent replacement. Certain other consumer products seem made to order for account management. Consider these industries in which some businesses have switched to consumer account management.

1. Luxury cars. The showroom sales force doubles as telemarketers. Several weeks after a sale the account representative calls the new owner to see how the car is performing. Each time periodic maintenance is due, the representative makes a courtesy call to remind the client. After two years, the representative calls to explain the features of the new models and offers to drop off a car for the client to test drive for several days.

2. Upscale clothing. The account representative makes note of each client's preferences and calls to alert the client when new merchandise arrives. If the merchandise is very expensive, the representative can arrange a private fitting in the client's office or home.

3. Gourmet foods. The account representative calls periodically to take orders and discuss the client's needs. When new products are introduced, the representative calls to explain them and offers to send a sample.

OTHER CONSUMER SALES

Consumer products which do not meet the criteria of high profit margin and recurring sales can still be sold by phone, but the telemarketer will not function as an account representative. After each prospect makes a purchasing decision, the telemarketer moves on to the next person.

DESIGNING A PRODUCT
FOR TELEMARKETING

Imagine buying a piece of equipment by three different methods: buying it in a store, buying it from a traveling representative, or ordering it over the phone. Depending on how you bought the equipment, the installation and repair procedures will be different *and the product itself may need design changes.*

If you buy a machine in a store, the clerk can demonstrate the proper operation and explain how to install it. If you buy it from a traveling representative, he or she can even install it for you. But if you buy it by phone, no one can physically demonstrate or install the machine.

A malfunction in the machine creates a similar distinction. The store may be able to repair the machine on the spot, may swap it for one in good repair, or may send it off to be fixed. A traveling salesperson can perform the same functions, but if you bought it by phone, you must either fix it yourself or ship it somewhere.

These complications illustrate a key design concept: for telemarketing to work, both the product and the service network must be user-friendly. If company representatives will install the product, it matters little whether the installation instructions are clear or confusing. If the customer must install it, the instructions must be completely clear and unambiguous.

To make installation easier, the product itself may need to be redesigned. A professional installer can splice wires together with connectors and a crimping tool, but most consumers would feel more confident making the connection at a screw terminal with a screwdriver.

Before starting a telephone campaign, management should examine the product itself, the associated literature, and the service and support network to ensure they are compatible with telemarketing.

The Product Itself: Is the product user-friendly, both for operation and repair? Are all controls logically placed and clearly marked? Can the unit be installed with simple tools? Can the unit be taken apart easily for repairs? Are model numbers and other essential information easy to find and easy to read?

The Associated Literature: Are all instructions so clear no one can misinterpret them? Have the instructions been tested to see if people unfamiliar with the product can follow them without hesitating or asking for advice? We believe strongly that companies outside the technical writing field should either contract with an outside technical writing firm or hire an experienced technical writer with a proven track record. Being able to write grammatical sentences does not guarantee a person can write clear instructions.

The Service and Support Network: Any product more complicated than sugar cookies will generate questions. Before the products reach the customers, the company must have some system for fielding those questions. For an operation which uses account representatives, they may be the logical people to field the questions, but they need to have answers to the obvious questions posted in front of them.

Questions about malfunctions or repairs can be more logically fielded by a service department, but that department also needs to be prepared. A technician who is skilled at bench repairs may not be adept at gleaning information and describing repair procedures over long-distance lines.

DESIGNING FOR CREDIBILITY

A potential weakness in a phone-first approach to new prospects is the universal worry about whether to trust the caller, the company, and the product. "How can I avoid getting caught in a scam sooner or later if I trust strangers on the telephone?" As telemarketing has grown, this reasonable fear has also grown, fed in part by investigative reporters on network TV and major wire services.

In the long-term, every organization involved in telemarketing should do everything possible to defeat telephone scams. Companies can distribute information to consumers, report scams, and participate in drafting sensible legislation to control telephone fraud.

In the short-term, a company which does not have clear name recognition with the prospect will have to plan a strategy to increase trust. At a minimum, if your organization is to sell by phone, it should have an ironclad guarantee: if the customer is not happy for any reason, he or she can get a full refund.

While both the authors of this book insist on an iron-clad guarantee in every telemarketing campaign, they differ on the role of the guarantee in promotion. Walter believes the guarantee should be downplayed; if the guarantee is pushed as a key point in the campaign some people will buy for the wrong reasons. Someone might buy an industry directory, copy key pages, and return it. Walter believes the guarantee should be present, but downplayed, to avoid the risk of excessive, costly returns.

Ray believes the guarantee should be prominent. While that policy does encourage some people to buy for the wrong reasons, the increased sales from skeptical prospects will more than offset the returns.

Depending on the guarantee alone will probably not be enough to offset widespread fears of a scam. Managers should look at all the ways to increase the information available to a customer and increase the customer's control over potential consequences.

If a person gets one marketing call from IBM and another from Albemarle Computers, the credibility problem is more likely to come up with Albemarle. Knowing that, a manager can do things to "look like IBM" or "look established." The synergistic approach discussed in the preceding chapter will not only increase awareness of the company and its product, but will create an impression that the company is well-established. Their logic is suspect, but many people act as though a company which runs radio spots and sends letters in addition to phone calls is less likely to take the money and run.

"Looking established" also means every letter and brochure must look professional. Too many companies raise questions about their staying power by sending letters printed on 9-pin dot matrix printers, or sending brochures with murky photocopied pictures, or including sentences which are nonsensical or grammatically suspect.

On the positive side, a company can increase credibility through the intelligent use of references. Every account executive should be trained to ask all satisfied customers if they can be used as references. To get a written reference, ask the customer what benefits she liked best about the product. Then mention you would like to share these benefits with others and ask if you could draft a short letter for her signature. Because you are doing all the work, most people feel open to this approach.

Increasing the customer's control over potential consequences requires careful planning based on a particular product and organization. We have seen how Sweet Caress Candy increased the margin of safety with a new product by delivering half the initial caseload and allowing the other half of the order to be changed without penalty.

Requiring prepayment before shipping can lessen the seller's risk and improve cash-flow but restrict sales. Delivering the product with an invoice allows the customer to inspect and use the product before committing any money.

With large lots or high unit prices, a significant cash-flow problem can develop for the seller if goods are delivered first for payment later. The Quick Response Technique used by the Australian Outback Collection among others offers a way to calm prospect's nerves without creating a cash-flow problem. In this approach products are shipped in very small lots (four men's coats, two hats) with payment on delivery. If those items sell, additional shipments can be made every other day. The Quick Response Technique requires more work, but it soothes anxiety by providing a smooth cash flow on both sides of the transaction.

Any one of these techniques makes sense only as part of a complete integrated strategy, since changing one part of the campaign often affects the other parts. For example, a strategy which includes sending free samples will have less need for inspection on delivery.

The bottom line: credibility does not just happen; it must be designed into the program at the beginning.

TESTING FOR
RESULTS

Although the original plan for integrating telephone selling with a specific product is largely intuitive, dramatic changes in marketing approaches and sometimes even in product and pricing can be instigated within weeks based on what occurs during the early calls.

The strength of interactive telemarketing is its ability to gather information while selling a product. Callers present benefits tailored to a particular prospect list while at the same time listening for legitimate objections and asking questions to dig as deeply as possible into the logic behind the criticism.

As the callers relay written and oral reports, the telemarketing manager can make changes to exploit unexpected strengths and correct weaknesses. Professional telemarketers sometimes speak of "the first hundred phone calls" referring to the test period of a campaign. Presumably in a hundred calls a manager can tell what works and what needs to be changed. Actually, the number is arbitrary; a highly responsive prospect list could demonstrate the success of the approach in thirty calls. On the other hand, a projected sales ratio of 3% would require a large sample to allow valid projections.

The number of calls is less important than the concept. After the campaign has been running for a day or two, the manager must sit down with the callers and evaluate the responses. Even a successful campaign can frequently be improved if the staff examines every element: "Do you hear much price resistance?" "Is there an easier way to explain the three for two bonus?" "Are you picking up some needs we didn't anticipate?"

CHANGING TO REMOTE
INVENTORIES

In business-to-business telemarketing, acceptance of the remote inventory concept is critical. If an outside sales force has been going in person to inventory each site, traditional clients may feel any change is a cut in service.

To smooth the transition to remote inventorying, lay the groundwork with these four steps:

1. Send a letter to all customers, explaining the benefits of a remote inventory system. Most customers like the system because it is less intrusive and responds quicker.

2. Set up a perpetual inventory system with easy access for you and the customer.

3. Allow plenty of time to retrain the old field sales force for remote inventories. Soothe wounded egos.

4. Develop and pretest all elements of the system: phone, mail or fax, computer, and printed order/inventory forms.

5. During the transition period, walk each customer through the entire process.

One of the simplest approaches is to develop an easy to use order form which can be faxed or filled out simultaneously by an account representative and a customer as they talk on the phone. The representative and the customer set up a short inventory cycle (weekly intervals, perhaps). At a set point in the cycle the account representative pulls a current inventory out of the computer and mails or faxes it and the order form to the customer. He follows with a call to discuss the next order. The representative can also use the computer to predict anomalies in the customer's purchasing pattern: "Last Memorial Day you had a run on do-it-yourself kits; should we increase the stock levels?"

KEY POINTS

1. Any company doing business-to-business selling through a traveling sales force needs to consider converting this operation to telemarketing.

2. Most activities traditionally performed by a traveling representative (inventory, for example) can now be done by phone or other remote means.

3. Videotapes, models, and samples can effectively replace face-to-face demonstrations of a new product.

4. Account management can be an effective approach for consumer products which have high profit margins and need periodic replacement.

5. Maximum effectiveness in telemarketing requires that the product itself, the associated literature, and the service and support network be designed with telemarketing in mind.

6. Credibility is critical because the public fears telephone scams.

7. To gain credibility, a company must have a solid money-back guarantee, send out professional letters and brochures, and collect references from established customers.

8. The telemarketing manager and staff must evaluate and adapt every campaign using data from the first few days.

9. Established customers need to be carefully prepared and walked through a change to remote inventories.

CHAPTER 6

TRACKING PROSPECTS: MAKE THE GOOD ONES BETTER

You can have a telemarketing staff that's loaded with talent—sensitive to clients' needs, articulate and confident, adept at overcoming objections, brimming with product knowledge, and skilled at picking the perfect moment to close each sale—overall, a great sales team; but if those people keep haphazard records on legal pads or 3x5 cards, every account will be a struggle after the first phone call. Worse yet, caller's will be wasting resources making repeated phone calls to poor prospects.

Inexperienced callers may believe they will never forget critical information about customers, but 50 calls a day will blur anyone's memory. Couple that with the effort required to retain facts for months between call-backs and the need for records becomes obvious.

Even more important is the need for organizational continuity. In Chapter Eleven we discuss strategies for combating turnover, but some turnover is inevitable. What happens when a good telemarketer leaves? If he kept good records, someone else can pick up his accounts easily. If he kept poor records, important accounts may fall through the cracks.

WHY RECORD
BAD PROSPECTS?

The A to D prospect classifications, discussed in Chapter Two are critical in record keeping, and should be an important element in staff training programs.

Someone once asked us: "If there are prospects that you believe you may never phone again—the Dog 4s—why waste time writing them up? Isn't that carrying thoroughness too far, just for the sake of thoroughness?"

This question has several answers:

1. Without any records, someone on the same campaign may call or mail to the same bad prospects again.

2. If no one records the reasons prospects refuse to buy, the campaign can't be refined. The staff may call other prospects with the same unworkable pitch.

3. Without information, you can't improve the mailing list for future use.

4. All ratings of prospects are temporary. Last year's impossible class D prospect can be this year's biggest customer for any number of reasons including personnel changes, new corporate objectives, better cash flow, or unhappiness with another supplier. When last year's D prospect calls to discuss an order, information from last year's phone call suddenly becomes critical.

PAPER OR
COMPUTER?

The Effect on Productivity: The seemingly endless expansion of telemarketing in the 1980s was matched (sometimes preceded) by an expansion of electronic tools. The capabilities of these tools range from modest to incredible—so do the prices, but none of them can solve basic strategy problems. If a staff member can make

30 calls a day with a simple headset and paper forms for record keeping, switching to computer records and some form of automatic dialing might increase the staffer's output to 40 calls. However, if the staffer is not closing any sales, buying equipment to speed up the process will simply exhaust the calling list faster.

Moral: If you can't close sales with a telephone, you can't close sales with a computer and a telephone.

The opposite is also true. A telemarketing operation which works well with telephones and headsets will run faster, easier, and often less expensive with computer support.

Database Software: Among the most basic of the new electronic tools is a telemarketing database, a computerized record system. Anyone with at least an MS-DOS or Macintosh computer will have a wide choice of software for record keeping.

Most of these programs are flexible enough for various applications. In a typical program, a telemarketer can call a client or prospect's record on the screen, study previous notes, push a button to automatically dial the number, make additional notes while talking, compose a follow-up letter, and create a reminder which will come up automatically when the next call to that client is due.

The same database can be used for mass mailings and, in certain versions, for filling orders and invoicing. The most sophisticated systems merge order-filling with the other operations. While talking with the client the telemarketer enters the quantity for an order and pushes a command key; the system then automatically creates a shipping order and invoice (and routes them electronically if the shipping department and accounts receivable are tied to the computer).

The advantages of telemarketing software over a conventional computer database are so great anyone with the required hardware should seriously consider a telemarketing database. Note: these programs are described by a number of generic titles including sales management packages, database marketing, account management systems, and sales activity databases. The choices are vast. Anyone seriously in the market should check the features of a number of competing programs.

For someone who must buy the computer(s) as well as the software, deciding whether to automate is a harder choice, but the benefits for a large-scale operation seem overwhelming.

A small telemarketing operation which is running well and expanding would also benefit from an investment in electronic tools. Buying one mid-sized computer and hooking a number of terminals into it may well cost as much as adding another staff member. However, increasing the efficiency of an already productive staff might generate more additional sales than adding a new employee.

A word of caution: having a telemarketing database does not make someone a good record-keeper. A telemarketer who keeps haphazard records on paper will be just as sloppy at a computer terminal. In either case the answer is better training or tighter staff discipline.

Learning About Equipment Options: Every month new telemarketing products with expanded capabilities appear. Merely listing and explaining all the available features would require more space than is available in this book. However, two options deserve special mention. In an organization with more than half a dozen callers, a good predictive dialing system will greatly speed up operations. This type of system will call numbers from a list, screening out (and annotating) busy signals, disconnected phones, no answers, and answering machines. When a human being answers, the system distributes the call to an available telemarketer and at the same time provides pertinent information on the computer screen.

Another popular option assists telemarketing managers in monitoring performance by providing an automatic printed summary of every call made from every station. The system discourages employees from making personal calls at company expense, allows the manager to spot and assist slow callers, and provides valuable statistics for planning work schedules at peak periods. This type of system is sometimes called SMDR for Station Message Detail Recorder.

For a quick look at a wide array of state of the art tools that support sales and marketing, consult *Future$ell: Automating Your Sales Force* by Ronald S. Kauffman (Boulder, CO: Cross Communications, 1990). To stay abreast of technological advances which support telemarketing and related activities consider reading one or both of the leading magazines in this area:

INBOUND/OUTBOUND
12 West 21 Street
New York, NY 10010
800-999-0345 (U.S.)
212-691-8215 (International)
212-691-1191 (FAX)

Telemarketing
One Technology Plaza
Norwalk, CT 06854
800-243-6002 (U.S.)
203-852-6800 (U.S. and International)
203-853-2845 (FAX)

From time to time each magazine will include a list of all systems and suppliers.

Throughout the rest of this chapter we will be discussing paper records, but the same functions must be performed, the same principles applied, and the same choices made with an electronic system.

PLANNING
THE SYSTEM

Whatever the format, a good telemarketing record system will have three basic components: basic information about the customer or prospect, a record of calls made with their results, and a reminder system for insuring future calls are made on time.

The Customer Record: In a paper system, the customer or prospect record needs to be in a form that is easy to access and change. Index cards are a possibility if you are calling through a list only one time, but traditional account management requires more space for notations. Most organizations use pre-printed sheets of paper filed in Manila folders.

The format for these printed sheets is infinitely variable, but we believe any effective record system will include these elements:

1. Company name.

2. Address.

3. Decision-maker's:

    a. Name.

    b. Title.

    c. Voice phone number.

    d. Fax number.

    e. Mailstop.

    f. Best calling hours.

4. Gatekeepers' names. (Gatekeepers are people, such as receptionists and personal secretaries, who control access to the decision-maker.)

5. Specific product needs and interests.

An effective customer record system will also have a number of elements tailored to the particular industry or market and the needs of the telemarketing staff. In designing the customer record sheet consider these possibilities:

1. Initials of the person who completes the sheet.

2. Credit information on the customer.

3. Tax exempt status and number(s).

4. Federal Identification Number(s).

5. Operating locations.

6. Number of years in business.

7. Credit limit and credit terms.

8. Bank/trade references.

A good mailing list will include some of this information; the rest can be collected from the customer.

Unless all customers were very similar, you would want to collect background information about the customer's business:

1. Type of business.

2. Types of jobs/services.

3. Typical clients or customers (municipal, industrial, state, etc.).

4. Other suppliers.

5. Desired shipping arrangements.

6. Typical promotions.

7. Peak seasons.

8. Special requirements.

Depending on the industry, you would probably want some information about the customer's needs relative to your product. If you were selling advertising for a string of retirement community newspapers, for instance, you might need this information on the form:

1. Customer's products targeted at the elderly.

2. Types of advertising used in the past.

3. Principal geographic market.

4. Does the customer need help designing ads?

We also recommend information about the particular person(s) with whom a telemarketer will be dealing.

1. Previous successes (related to ours or competitors' products).

2. Previous problems.

3. What do they value most in a supplier?

    a. Quick delivery.

      b. Low price.

      c. Broad Inventory.

      d. Technical expertise.

      e. Easy access (good hours, open phone lines).

      f. Assistance in promotions.

      g. Reliable products.

      h. Other.

4. Family information.

5. Friends in common.

6. Conversational style. (Is it concise and to the point, or relaxed and friendly?)

7. Voice qualities. (So no one has to say, "Is this Frank?")

Items 4 and 5 on the above list sometimes cause raised eyebrows. After all, isn't this a business enterprise instead of a gossip line? When you see a marketing note that indicates that when your staffer called, Mr. Smith was leaving the office for a funeral is that notation a poor use of paper and time? Is your sales representative getting too personal?

In considering these questions, we need to remember people don't buy because they hear a canned sales pitch; they buy because they trust the seller. Relationships matter in selling and are doubly important in a long buying cycle or a long-term account. If a sympathy card after a funeral, or the mention of a vacation, or a not too personal question about recovery from an illness will help cement a business relationship, your staffers should be encouraged to pursue these avenues. Here, as elsewhere, records are critical.

Whatever the format, customer records need to be filed in some logical order. Alphabetically within market segments works well. One of our systems is a good illustration. Ray segments government clients by branch of government and business clients by geographic area. His filing categories are:

— Air Force
— Army
— Prison System
— [Other] Federal Government
— State and Local Government
— Colorado Businesses
— Out-of-state Businesses
— International Clients

Depending on how your business is structured, the same folders can hold copies of orders, invoices, quotations, proposals, and correspondence.

Customer records also need easy to read and easy to change markings for prospect classifications (A, B, C, D). Colored stickers are the easiest method.

The Record of Calls: Basic information about the customer is not enough. The caller must also know what was said and who agreed to what on previous calls. This information may be kept separately or may be a part of the customer record. Some managers insist on separate sheets to provide an easily scanned record of each telemarketer's work.

In some systems the caller or the computer records all calls made by that caller in a single list, regardless of who was called. This system makes recording easy and allows easy comparisons of work done by different callers, but it makes retrieving information about a particular client difficult. We do not recommend this type of single list unless the caller or computer duplicates information in customer records.

The basic information for a call record is very simple:

1. Customer name and account number.

2. Date of call.

3. Name of person with whom the caller spoke.

4. Result of call. ("He will send purchase order ASAP." "Promised to fax our rate schedule.")

5. Future action. ("Call after federal budget passes." "She will call after surveying their clients.")

Either the Customer Record or the Record of Calls must include a list of literature sent to the customer. A caller who has to ask, "Did we send you our new price sheet?" is betraying a lack of organization in your company.

The Reminder System: With only a few accounts a telemarketer can scan the call records to see which call-backs to make on a given day, but most operations are too large for that. The solution is a variation on the familiar office tickler cards or suspense file.

Whatever the system is called, it consists of a file box with dividers or a file with Manila folders. In either case, the segments are labeled 1 to 31, for the days of the month, and January through December. After each completed call, the caller marks on a card or paper the customer's name, prospect classification, and date to call. The cards/sheets may be printed or blank so long as everyone knows how to use them.

Calls to make during the current month are filed under the appropriate date. Other calls are filed under the month name. On the first of each month the caller pulls all the cards or sheets for that month and refiles them by date.

At the end of each day, the caller pulls reminders for the next day and sorts them by classification since it is more important to complete call-backs to "A" clients than to "C" clients. With an auto-dialing phone, some callers like to program numbers at this point. On the next day the caller simply makes the call-backs in order, pulling the customer record and call record to review before each call.

FEEDBACK TO MANAGEMENT

A good record system benefits the organization as well as the individual telemarketer, but only if the organization gets the information. In a small operation, the manager can stay on top of things by chatting with each caller frequently and by reviewing the records periodically. A large organization may need a more formal system, perhaps a form (paper or computer) with categories like new applications, additional prospects, significant objections, and other. Any caller who picks up information management needs to know scribbles it on the form and sends it up.

The secret to making any feedback system work is atmosphere. If a caller ever perceives that management is irritated at the interruption feedback creates, that source of feedback will dry up, no matter how simple the system is.

KEEPING THE
STAFF ORGANIZED

Staff members who keep poor records can cripple an operation, but good record-keeping is hard and unrewarding work. To ensure quality records, a manager needs to train well, monitor closely, and reward liberally.

Training Record-keeping: Trainees need to know not only how the record system operates, but why it operates. For new people the payoff is rarely self-evident; the trainer may want to walk them through some horror stories:

> A large client organization has several buyers in their contracting department. One of these buyers tells the telemarketer he will place a large order when the new quarter begins. Two months later the telemarketer calls back, but can't remember which buyer made the promise. Instead of confidently asking, "How many gross shall we ship?" he must ask, "Are you the person I spoke to about ordering widgets?"

> One telemarketer calls a Navy base which is expected to complete a large service contract. She learns that the Secretary of the Navy has frozen all funds for non-essential services, but she neglects to relay that information. Other telemarketers spend days getting the runaround from other bases which are less forthright.

A telemarketer makes an appointment to call back on the first of the month but forgets to put a card in the tickler file. A month later he calls back and learns the ex-customer has place a large order with a competitor.

Monitoring Record-keeping: The kind of people who make good telemarketers enjoy engaging people on the phone and thrill at closing a sale. They are not excited about keeping records. Given that emotional tilt, training alone is rarely enough to achieve the quality records required for a long-term operation.

To keep everyone attentive to the organization's needs, we recommend periodically reviewing the records of every caller. One workable system consists of daily reviews of the call records and monthly reviews of the customer records.

Rewarding Record-keeping: A piece of negative information that gets a campaign back on track may be more valuable than any single sale. Managers should recognize that and reward staffers who take the time to document carefully. If you applaud sales leaders, you should also recognize people who feedback valuable information.

Since any organization tends to get what it pays for, a smart manager will examine the compensation system to see what value is placed on keeping records. If the staff only gets money for completed calls or closed sales, no amount of jawboning will get them to slow down and keep records. A well-documented refusal from a Class D prospect may not be worth as much as a sale, but it is worth something if it prevents wasted resources in the future. The compensation system should reflect that fact.

RECORD-KEEPING WITH RELUCTANT PROSPECTS

New accounts can create a problem if the caller needs to collect information but the client is reluctant. The caller must be inquisitive without seeming to pry into proprietary information. Part of the secret is timing. Credit information is sensitive but not necessary until the prospect is ready to open an account. Other information will always be sensitive. Sweet Caress Candy may want to be sure a distributor is stocked with Praline Puffs before the distributor's next big promotion, but the distributor may be trying to steal a march on his competitors by keeping the promotion secret. Conflicts like this can only be resolved if both parties trust each other.

Managers need to coach their telemarketers to prevent alienating potential customers with heavy-handed questioning. Callers need to be prepared to back off if they sense resistance to certain questions.

Sometimes an adept telemarketer can disarm resistance in advance.

"I want to find out as much about your company as I can. But I don't want information that you would consider secret or proprietary, because I would not want you to believe I gave away information you told me in confidence."

Strangely, this advance statement often clears the way for callers to receive a certain amount of information that must be kept in confidence. Because the caller showed she was sensitive to the need for secrecy, the prospect was able to relax and share necessary information.

MAKING GOOD PROSPECTS BETTER

Keeping good records is never an end in itself. Careful records help winnow the wheat from the chaff by flagging questionable prospects and aid astute telemarketers in making good prospects or customers into better ones.

Previous call records help a telemarketer build relationships by asking questions about the buyer's vacation, or the daughter who got a job with the airlines.

Customer records help a telemarketer anticipate the customer's upcoming needs, thus establishing a superior reputation for customer service.

The reminder system helps telemarketers meet every appointment promptly, reinforcing the company image of timely responses.

Taken together, these systems gradually distinguish a superior marketing operation from the mediocre ones and draw the customer into your corner.

KEY POINTS

1. Even the best telemarketers can't rely on memory alone.

2. Good records ensure continuity in the face of turnover.

3. Poor prospects need to be documented to avoid wasting additional resources.

4. A number of good computer systems are available for keeping records, but the same information is needed whether it is kept on paper or a computer disk.

5. Vital information about each customer is kept in a customer record with calls annotated on a call record.

6. Every system needs some form of reminder to jog the memory of callers when call-backs are due. Cards filed by day of the month for the present month and by name of the month for future months are the most common.

7. To ensure quality records, a manager needs to train the staff in record-keeping, monitor the records closely, and reward the staffers who keep good records and feedback important information.

8. Good records allow the company to respond consistently to customer needs and, thus, improve customer relations.

CHAPTER 7

ESTABLISHING COURTESY AS A BENCHMARK

UNAVOIDABLE RUDENESS

The telephone has an element of built-in rudeness. Nowhere is this better illustrated than in Philip Mahfood's fanciful example of a man desperately trying to defend his work to his boss, who has just entered his office with criticism of a major project.

> "Suddenly, literally out of nowhere—a person who was not there one second earlier jumps on his desk, pushes aside his project, steps between him and the boss, and starts talking without so much as an 'excuse me'!
> You have just conjured up a typical business phone call." (Philip E. Mahfood, *Teleselling*, Probus Publishing, Chicago, 1990.)

COURTESY AS POLICY

We have all been interrupted by the phone, and many of us have a lingering sense of irritation whenever it rings. The key to soothing that irritation and developing solid business relationships is (obviously) courtesy. To establish a positive company image and distance their programs from tiresome boiler-room tactics, managers must make telephone courtesy a top priority.

Hiring Courteous People: Basic courtesy is so important that many telemarketing managers will only hire people in whom it is second nature. Unfortunately, many people who are the soul of courtesy in face-to-face encounters are inadvertently rude on the phone—thus, the need for training.

Avoiding the Pressure Cooker: Even worse are ill-advised management policies which sacrifice courtesy for quota pressure. When a Simon Legree approach by management insists that the phoner is not likely to succeed on less than 150 calls a day, courtesy is usually the first victim and employee morale the second.

There's no room in a strong telemarketing program for a burned out telephone sales representative, or one who is jaded as a result of poor training and impossible quotas in somebody's boiler room. So how do managers get adults who are talented but hardened to telephone work to make courtesy a cornerstone of their work?

They start by avoiding the pressures inherent in so many boiler-room operations. When that term came in vogue between the world wars, many fly-by-night operations were in the cheapest available space, the basement boiler rooms of run-down buildings. Desks and phones were crowded together, lighting was bad and the dwellers in these dungeons were baked by the boilers. Those days are gone, but it is surprising how many phone rooms today are laid out in tiny, sterile cubicles, de-emphasizing the human values that allow telemarketers to patiently build the relationships that spell permanence and profits.

A Pleasant Place to Work: The requirements for a good work environment are really very simple. Every telemarketer should have a private space which is pleasant and comfortable. It should be quiet, well lighted, and equipped with all the necessary tools: desk, comfortable chair, filing cabinet or computer terminal, telephone with headset, calendar, area code and time zone maps, and fact sheets on the product. We want staffers who will stay at their posts and keep calling for long hours and still come across as relaxed and confident on the last call every day. They can't do that if the workplace is too hot, too cold, too noisy, too cramped, or smoke-filled.

Incidentally, a noisy space not only wears down the callers, it creates an unprofessional image. A prospect who hears background noise on the phone is likely to envision the ever-familiar boiler room.

Management must also have reasonable policies, set attainable goals, and pay competitive salaries. Teaching the techniques for telephone courtesy is only part of the task. The fundamental requirements are hiring courteous, happy people and providing them a place where they will enjoy working.

PRINCIPLES AND GUIDELINES

Curbing Old Habits: Having secured a good work environment staffed with good people, the manager needs to establish guidelines for approaching customers and clients with courtesy. People who are courteous by nature are often unaware that certain of their phone habits can be irritating. Outside of the business world people are rarely taught anything about how to talk on the phone, so they ordinarily give no thought to it. Consider this normal teenage conversation:

"Hello."

"Janet?"

"Yeah."

"So, whatcha doing?"

"Who's this?"

"Frieda—from band."

"Oh, yeah."

Probably neither girl in this conversation would find anything rude about it. After completing high school and a few years in non-telephone jobs, their vocabulary will be different, but without training, their basic approach is likely to be the same:

"Hello."

"I'm looking for Joe."

"You got him."

"O.K. . . So, how are you today?"

(very guarded) "I'm O.K."

"Good. Do you ever need any lightbulbs? See, I'm with the Junction City Brigade for Better Sidewalks, and we are calling families to see if they need stuff."

"Do I know you?"

"I just got your name from a list. My name is Frieda."

Frieda may be smart, well-educated, and charming, even articulate in other circumstances, but in this call she has come across as disorganized, unduly familiar, and inconsiderate of the prospect's time. A manager would do well to take nothing for granted. A competent, hard-working, ambitious recruit may be totally ignorant of fundamental telephone manners. Everyone who owns a phone has received irritating calls from people trying to sell various products. The first question in most of these calls is "How are you today?" That question is irritating on two counts: it wastes time, and it implies familiarity. Most of us do not want to make small talk with strangers before we know what they want.

Most inexperienced telemarketers have been irritated by that very question, but most of them will still use it unless they are coached. Take nothing for granted.

Basic Principles: A smart manager will ensure the staff understands the philosophy behind company policy. In the realm of telephone courtesy that philosophy is best expressed in three principles:

1. Respect the customer's time.

2. Respect the customer's privacy.

3. Respect the customer's integrity.

Guidelines: Most of the actions courteous callers take seem self-evident, but the staff needs to hear about them anyway. One person who is unaware of his or her obnoxious habits can damage a company's image beyond repair. A manager should not only teach but monitor these guidelines:

1. Always treat receptionists, assistants, and secretaries with respect, even if you are sure they are screening you from the decision-maker. Today's assistant may be tomorrow's decision-maker, and the power of some secretaries is legendary. Learn the names of these people, and after the first call chat with them about their interests.

2. Always identify yourself before saying anything else. Your name alone will suffice for a receptionist; with a decision-maker you should identify your organization: "I'm Jan Anderson from Sweet Caress Candy."

3. Ask for the decision-maker by name: "I'm Jan Anderson calling for Inigo Montes." Try to avoid the tentative request: "May I speak to _____?"

4. If you don't know the decision-maker's name, get it from the receptionist: "I need the name of your Director of Human Resources." If you ask to speak to the director, you will be connected without having a chance to get the name.

5. Use the form of the name as it is given to you or address the decision-maker by title and last name. If the decision-maker answers, "This is Jennifer Baker," you can call her Ms. Baker, or Dr. Baker, or Jennifer—but never Jenny. Never use a nickname unless she uses it.

6. When speaking to anyone, use his or her name frequently. Dale Carnegie said the sweetest sound in the English language is the sound of a man's own name.

7. Don't waste the other person's time. When you reach a decision-maker for the first time, state your basic idea immediately. "Jennifer, I'm Jan Anderson from Sweet Caress Candy. We are introducing a low-calorie whipped praline for the holiday season, and I can offer you, not only a large discount on your first offer, but a free demographic analysis of candy buyers in your area." Once you have the person's interest, small talk may be helpful in building a relationship.

8. After getting across your basic idea, ask if the other person has time to talk. If not, make an appointment to call back.

9. Never use profanity. Not even with the purchasing agent for this year's funkiest rock group. You can't risk losing clients by guessing how they will react.

10. Never let on you don't believe what someone is saying, even if it is patently false. Our object is to make sales, not score debating points.

11. Treat disagreements as misunderstandings.

12. Listen carefully.

13. Never talk about one customer to another customer.

14. When you determine someone will never buy the product, do not just say "thank you" curtly and hang up. Instead, say, "I do appreciate your taking the time to listen to me." Remember, customers talk to each other. If you sound abrupt, the word will get around.

15. If you promise to send something such as a letter, catalog, or price sheet, arrange for it as soon as you complete your notes from the phone call and make certain it goes out that day. Promptness is a form of courtesy.

16. Make tactful follow-up calls. When you make these calls, the decision-maker may regard you as a pest or a welcome calendar secretary. To avoid being a pest, ask the decision-maker for a good time to call again; then preface the new call with "When we talked last _____, you wanted me to check back this week."

REACHING THE DECISION-MAKER

The familiar obstacles in reaching someone by phone can cause a breakdown in courtesy. A good training program will equip callers with the tools needed to negotiate the obstacles without losing their cool.

Obstacle—the Busy Line: Callers need to put a busy signal in the right perspective. If the line is busy that normally means the decision-maker is there—no need for telephone tag. We have found that calling back exactly eight minutes after the first call will frequently find the person still in the office but off the phone.

Obstacle—In Conference: "Mr. Rashid is in a conference; can he call you back?" The caller should try to keep the initiative by one of these methods:

> WALTER'S RESPONSE: "I'll be happy to call Mr. Rashid back. Your voice is much nicer than my busy signals! How soon do you think he might be available?"

> RAY'S RESPONSE: "I'm going to be in and out, so it would be easier if I called him. When would be a good time?"

Obstacle—Out of Town: "Mr. Wu is out of town. If you'll give me your phone number, I'll have him call you back as soon as he's back in the office." This one is tougher, but the caller should still try to call back rather than waiting for a call which never comes or being caught off guard by a call at a bad time.

> WALTER'S RESPONSE: "I'll be happy to call Mr. Jones back at his convenience, because your voice is much nicer than my busy signals. If you'll tell me when he'll be back, I'll note it and call him a few days after he returns so that he has a chance to catch up on old business before I confront him with something new."

RAY'S RESPONSE: "It would be easier for me to call him. When do you expect him back in the office?"

If the caller needs a decision before the end of the trip, she should ask if someone else can make the decision or else accept the risks of a return call at the decision-maker's convenience.

Obstacle—Never Available: The caller makes a series of calls and hears an excuse each time. "Mrs. Washington is away from her desk. . . has just stepped out. . . is not available just now." Even if the caller suspects he is being shoved aside, he must remain calm and friendly as he tries to break the logjam by one of these methods:

1. Make an exception and accept a call-back at a specific time early or late in the day when the department phones are relatively inactive. The odds improve if the call can be arranged before or after normal hours.

2. Fax a short note to the decision-maker stating the main benefit of this offer and asking to set up a telephone appointment.

3. Handwrite a note using the method described in Chapter Four.

4. Send the secretary and the decision-maker something distinctive *which is connected with the offer.* A corporate travel agency could send a pass for a month's free parking at an airport shuttle lot.

Obstacle—Decision Relay: "Dr. Steiner is very busy. He would like you to tell me what you have in mind so I can relay it to him." This situation is very awkward for the caller but it leaves little choice. Something has to be said. The best approach is a brief, glowing description of the product's major benefits. The caller should leave out details, especially price. If the gambit works, the decision-maker will become interested and negotiate directly rather than relaying messages.

A less satisfactory, but still workable, solution is a continuous relay in which information in both directions is funneled through the secretary or assistant. The caller in this case must work to influence both the decision-maker and the intermediary (who is never completely neutral when relaying messages). The caller should also try to fax complex messages to avoid possible confusion in the relay.

Obstacle: No Time To Talk: The decision-maker says, "I'm sorry to interrupt. I really shouldn't have taken this phone call; I don't have any time to talk." The caller should respond: "Pat, I want to save your time too. Give me a convenient time for me to call back and in the meantime I'll send a fact sheet describing our three-for-the-price of-two-discount."

COURTESY WITH A COMMITTEE

If the prospect is a purchasing committee, courtesy suggests that all committee members be kept informed, but prudence dictates negotiating with only one member. The caller should try to talk to the same person each time (preferably the committee head), but should ask permission to address all members whenever a letter or mailing goes out.

COPING WITH FRUSTRATION

No Wasted Calls: The longer the day, the ruder the customers, the fewer the closings—the harder it is to maintain courtesy on the next call. To make courtesy more than a matter of sterile technique, the manager must work to keep everyone in the right frame of mind. Fundamental to that frame of mind is getting people to accept the fact that there are no wasted phone calls. A call to the wrong office still brings a caller one step closer to the right office. A busy signal means we finally know the prospect's location. A rejected offer provides information to refine the campaign. And rude, obnoxious responses from someone who will never buy provide a chance to practice coping skills for use with the gruff, overworked prospect who will buy.

Long-Distance Friends: Nothing is more potent for achieving courtesy and lessening the fear of cold calling than this bit of philosophy:

"These are not strangers I am calling; they are simply long-distance friends I haven't yet met."

KEY POINTS

1. Telephones are inherently irritating because they interrupt us, but well-trained, courteous telemarketers can soothe the irritation and establish solid business relationships.

2. Managers need to hire people who are naturally courteous, provide them a pleasant place to work, and protect them from unreasonable pressure.

3. Many people who are naturally courteous still have bad phone habits. A good manager will explain even the most fundamental concepts about courtesy on the phone.

4. A courteous telemarketer will respect the customer's time, privacy, and integrity.

5. Callers need to realize getting a busy signal puts them only one step away from a contact. Calling back in eight minutes will usually find the decision-maker in the office and off the phone.

6. Callers should make appointments to call the prospect back rather than accepting the secretary's invitation to have the prospect call.

7. If the prospect is never available, the caller needs to break the logjam somehow. Possibilities include accepting a call-back outside normal hours, sending a fax or a handwritten note, or sending something distinctive.

8. When dealing with a committee, the telemarketer should always call one person but send courtesy copies of correspondence to all members.

9. Courtesy is largely a state of mind. Callers should keep themselves in the right frame of mind by remembering there are no wasted calls. They can gain something from every call, even if it is just experience in dealing with difficult prospects.

CHAPTER 8

MINIMIZING CUSTOMER HOSTILITY

DENYING THE OBVIOUS

Positive Thinking: Many telemarketers will deny the existence of a hostile market even when they are in one. Why?

Few of us believe we can build anything of value in a negative climate. The idea of a hostile market poses a dilemma in a culture which idolizes positive thinking. How can anyone be successful selling to new customers if he believes they will reject him, his company, and his product? How can he avoid being sucked under by the quicksand of defeatism?

It is easier to believe friendliness will beget friendliness, but anyone who has spent a week calling new prospects knows how quickly the marketplace can become a jungle. Too often telemarketers are viewed as predators, who must be beaten back by verbal blows.

A telemarketer cannot prevail in the long run with a polyanna outlook. Everyone eventually encounters prospects so openly hostile their attitudes cannot be glossed over with wishful thinking. At that point the polyannas must either change or collapse in despair. The best of the telemarketing breed are tough enough to face hostility and overcome it.

Irrefutable Evidence: Charles Dickens in *A Christmas Carol* depicted the ghost of Jacob Marley dragging an immense chain fastened to ledgers, locks, and cash boxes, the symbols of his past sins. Every legitimate telemarketer wears a "Marley's Chain" of other people's sins, and must be prepared to combat being cast in a common mold with scam artists and nuisance callers. The antipathy of some citizens toward telemarketing is supported by ample evidence:

1. Millions of people pay several dollars a month to have unlisted telephone numbers. Even as this chapter was being written, one of the authors cancelled his business listing in the phone directory. The listing was not attracting any business but was bringing in many nuisance phone calls.

2. Millions more hire answering services or buy answering machines. A service or answering machine has several functions, but one of those is usually screening out unwanted calls.

3. Others have standing orders to secretaries and receptionists not to let any outside calls through.

One only has to listen to telemarketers' anecdotes about being snapped at and hung up on to realize not all sales resistance is benign.

CAUSES OF HOSTILITY

As we mentioned in the last chapter, almost everyone has some lingering irritation with the telephone and its interruptions. But hostility springs from a deeper, more virulent source manifested in patently offensive actions: sarcasm, baiting, ethnic slurs, yelling, profanity, other verbal abuse, and abrupt hangups.

What makes some markets so hostile, and why do telemarketers feel the hostility more than a traveling sales force? The key to both questions is the word "stranger." Most outside sales groups are organized by routes or territories. Each staff member is expected to call on a number of old customers and some new prospects. Since the percentage of cold calls is low and may depend on appointments, the sales rep rarely faces people unwilling to see him. What resistance he does face is buffered by travel time, so he can recover before seeing the next prospect.

How different life is for the telemarketer, who may be viewed as a stranger by 30-60 contacts every day. Anthropologists say the fear of strangers is a survival instinct lodged deep in the human psyche. That fear tends to flare up on the phone. Because we cannot see telephone callers we have difficulty judging their character and intentions.

Coupled with the fear of strangers is the fear of risk. For just reasons, everyone is wary of being suckered in telephone scams. A legitimate telemarketer can inadvertently say something which triggers recollections of a scam and the attack is on.

SHIFTING
THE BLAME

When a campaign is not going well, some managers (and even some callers) will start saying, "it's just a hostile market," even if it isn't.

When a telemarketing project is greeted with epidemic disdain, nine times in ten the program has highly identifiable flaws:

1. The product or service is poorly conceived and non-competitive.

2. The marketing or sales presentation lacks credibility or is so poorly organized and presented that prospects cannot understand what is being said or what is wanted of them.

3. The phone representatives are abrasive and discourteous.

4. The phone calls for this campaign sound just like all the others bombarding people in a saturated marketplace. Callers are not conveying a clear, *distinctive* benefit in the first sentence, so prospects feel they are being hounded again by "those sales people."

5. The program has no flexibility. No one is making mid-course corrections based on market feedback.

6. Callers are afraid to face legitimate customer objections. They use "hostile market" as an excuse to skip to the next name every time someone challenges them. A compensation system with rewards based on the number of calls made can encourage this behavior. Callers must remember every tough questioner is not a Class D prospect.

All of these factors are direct reflections on management. Anytime "hostile market" gets bandied about, the staff should turn introspective to see if they are trying to sidestep tough problems.

MINIMIZING HOSTILITY

Staff Philosophy: Forestalling hostility is better than overcoming it. To accomplish that, a staff needs to accept these principles:

1. If you try to sell something you don't believe in, the public has good reason to suspect a scam. To have the moral courage to deal with continued rejection and skepticism, telemarketers must believe they are performing a valuable public service and meeting genuine human needs.

2. The first time you talk with a potential buyer on the telephone, you're the remotest of strangers—especially in a program in which a telephone call is planned as the initial contact. As a stranger, your ethics are in question. Never do anything to cast doubt on your honesty or fairness. For that reason, callers should never "wing it" in response to a question. A better approach is, "I don't know the answer, but I will find out and get back with you."

3. The public is justified in its worries about fly-by-night operations. Pressuring a concerned prospect can create hostility. You would do better to rely on repeated contacts to establish your reliability.

Managers who get the best results from their staffs, and who have the lowest turnover statistics, feed these tenets to their marketing teams regularly, and skip the sugar-coated pills. Positive thinking and visions of success are powerful tools, but they must be tempered by reality. Rare is the campaign with no hostile prospects.

Improving List Management: Using calling lists which are inaccurate or redundant, or mismanaging a good list will definitely create resentment. One of the authors was composing this chapter at home on a word processor when he was forced to get up and cross the room to field this phone call:

"Hello."

"Mr. Gerdes?"

"My name is Ray Harlan. I think you want my step-son."

"Are you the man of the house?"

"Yes."

"Well, as a homeowner you are probably concerned about the value . . ."

"But I'm not a homeowner. We're renting until we can sell our other house."

"Well, thanks anyway."

CLICK.

The author, who is a calm, wonderful person, did not get hostile with this caller. (But he thought about it.) The caller made three basic mistakes:

1. He did not identify himself and his company (basic courtesy).

2. He wanted to sell a home improvement product to a sixteen-year-old (poor quality list).

3. He approached a family which did not own a home in that area (poor list again).

To avoid this type of problem, work from a recently updated list which is logical for the target market. To find homeowners, use a list compiled from tax records or people who have purchased home insurance. A list compiled from the phone book or a list of grocery store shoppers will be brimming with potential hostility.

Even a good list is likely to have redundancies. That's why we sometimes get three identical pieces of direct mail with slight variations in name or address. A computer can easily scrub a list and remove identical names and addresses, but removing names with slight variations is costly. Sending a few duplicate mailings is usually cheaper.

Getting three pieces of mail is not much of a problem as long as a wastebasket is handy. Getting three phone calls with the same salespitch can be maddening. To prevent this problem, callers can easily spot redundancies if they watch for them and if all the names are alphabetized in one list. Two listings for the same prospect will usually be consecutive. If the list is not alphabetized or if it is broken up into shorter segments (airline pilots, commercial pilots, private pilots, charter pilots) the task is much harder. After 200 calls, no one can remember if the next name matches one called three days ago.

The best approach for a long list with possible redundancies is to keep checking the call records. Anyone previously called should have a record.

Poor List Management—A Case Study: Bad list management was evident in the campaign to sell an industrial directory, which we discussed in Chapter Two.

As we mentioned, this project had a poorly designed script which tried to do too much, trying to verify listings and close sales with a single telephone call. Because of the pressure, callers were challenging prospects who did not want to purchase. Although printed information was offered to back up phone calls, this part of the operation was so poorly organized no sales person could be sure that everyone who was offered a mailing would receive it.

Each day, each caller would get copies of pages from the master prospect list with instructions to call a particular section of the alphabet. By a mix-up in assignments, some letters in the alphabet were covered by two or three callers. Prospects began to think the campaign had been organized to pressure them by repetitive phone calls into buying advertising, special listings, and books. By the third call for the same purpose, prospects were openly hostile. If by some miracle a sale was made, management could not accurately fix commission credits since several people could have made the calls.

Eventually, matters got even worse. Management separated the list-verifying function from the sales function and used two separate teams. With that system, as many as six persons identifying themselves with the directory company might contact a single prospect. The damage might have been lessened if one team had told prospects to expect another call, but without coordination, the right hand did not know what the left was doing. Talk about building hostility instead of sales. . . nothing could ever exceed this program.

The solution is obvious—think through how the list should be handled and stay organized. As we mentioned before, one of the benefits of an account representative system is lack of confusion: the prospect always talks to the same representative.

Battling the Scam Artist Legacy: Anytime someone is cheated by a voice on the telephone, all legitimate telemarketers are hurt. It follows that anyone involved in this business should do everything possible to stamp out illegal and unethical uses of the phone.

Since a prospect's hostility may be linked to a previous exposure with telephone fraud or abuse, every telemarketer needs the ability to distance this enterprise from the fraudulent or abusive ones. Helping a hostile prospect settle accounts with those who have cheated him is the best method for establishing your own legitimacy.

Here's how a telemarketer might pick up the hint:

> The prospect is agreeable and wants to purchase, but he suddenly get angry when the caller asks for his Master-Card number. The caller says, "apparently you are not comfortable giving me this number." It turns out the man had a lot of merchandise charged to his card by someone who called and said, "This is MasterCard International doing a random audit of cardholders. Would you mind verifying the number on your card? It begins 541. . . ." The

man then gave out his number, never realizing all Master-Cards begin with 541.

A telemarketer begins, "I'm Bill Ainsworth with the Central States Health Consortium. We would like to offer some free information about your children's health." The woman prospect angrily challenges him and asks for his credentials. Her anger stems from an incident the previous week when her daughter's ex-boyfriend decided to get even by having a friend call with this message: "I'm from the Center for Public Health. Please tell your daughter her AIDS test came out positive."

In order to offer timely assistance, callers need to be armed with information, typically addresses and phone numbers for the state attorney general, state utility commission, consumer protection agency, and Better Business Bureau for every area that will be called. The easiest source for most of this information is the *Consumer's Resource Handbook* published by the U.S. Office of Consumer Affairs. Single copies are free from:

The Consumer Information Center
Pueblo, CO 81009

Armed with this information, telemarketers can steer prospects to the agencies which will take action against telephone abuse. If a telemarketer wants to really win over a hostile prospect, she can take direct action by calling the appropriate agency for the prospect.

A scam in the distant past probably can't be corrected, but callers should help consumers understand how to defend themselves in the future. Sending out copies of the *Consumer's Resource Handbook* is a nice gesture.

Defusing Hostility: To deal with hostility, telemarketers must stay calm. Keeping the right perspective is the key; every telemarketer must be able to say, "This anger is the prospect's problem, not mine. I can let the prospect be angry while I stay calm."

Callers will also bear up better if they remember hostility offers an opportunity. If the problem behind the hostility can be solved, the prospect may become an extremely loyal customer.

If the hostile prospect issues a direct challenge, the caller should respond obliquely:

> "I know your game; it's lowball. Offer the sucker one good piece of merchandise as a bargain and then unload all the shoddy stuff when he isn't looking."

> *"My perspective is different.* We do offer an introductory special, but that's because we are convinced customers will appreciate both our prices and our quality merchandise." Avoid saying, "you're wrong."

If the prospect gets angry and abusive without stating the problem, the caller should try to draw him out:

> "Mr. McCoy, I need your help. Apparently I said something which offended you, but I don't know what it was. How can we get this conversation back on an even keel?"

Whatever the prospect says then, the caller should listen carefully and avoid discounting the prospect's feelings. ("You shouldn't feel that way" sounds innocuous but actually adds fuel to the fire.) If the problem can be solved, the caller should help solve it.

If a telemarketing campaign is well-designed and well-managed it should not be generating hostility. Therefore, if hostility occurs, it comes from another source such as previous unhappy experiences. If the source is exposed to daylight, the hostility may evaporate.

KEY POINTS

1. Many telemarketers would rather not believe it, but hostility toward telephone selling is frequent.

2. The two principle causes of hostility on the phone are fear of strangers and fear of risk.

3. When a campaign is not going well, some telemarketers will hide their own shortcomings by claiming "It's just a hostile market."

4. Telemarketers can often forestall hostility by believing in the value of what they are doing, admitting when they don't have an answer, and avoiding pressure tactics.

5. Using calling lists which are inaccurate or redundant or mismanaging a good list will definitely create resentment among prospects.

6. Legitimate telemarketers should help victims of telephone scams catch up with the perpetrators.

7. To defuse hostility, callers should stay calm, try to learn the source of the anger, and deal with the problem.

CHAPTER 9

MEETING OBJECTIONS AND CLOSING THE SALE

Every other skill in a caller's repertoire is useless unless the caller can overcome objections and close the sale. In general, telemarketing uses the same principles as face-to-face selling for overcoming objections and concluding sales. However, phone sales work poses an additional challenge because the buyer is always out of sight.

ASSESSING STAFF EXPERIENCE

The skills a telemarketer has for dealing with the unseen prospect are largely dependent on previous experience. For that reason, the telemarketing manager who must ensure the staff is competent to handle objections and closings should start by assessing staff experience.

Converting from Field Sales: A traveling sales staff converted to telemarketing will already understand objections and closings; studying the sometimes subtle differences between telephone and face-to-face work should let them make the basic adjustments.

Experienced Telemarketers: Telephone sales people hired from out-side, may have well developed skills at sensing objections, but may also have bad habits learned in a "hard sell" operation.

Inexperienced Sales Staff: Staff members new to sales will not have to unlearn hard sell tactics, but they will need to be taught every-thing else.

HOW SELLING BY PHONE DIFFERS FROM FACE-TO-FACE

Non-Vocal Cues: Telemarketing differs from face-to-face selling in several important ways. In a face-to-face pitch, physical actions and reactions—a smile, a nod, a relaxation of facial muscles, a gesture—often signal that the prospect is ready to make a purchase. A frown, a crossing of the arms, or dropping of eye contact could indicate an unspoken objection. The telemarketer gets none of those cues and can be misled at times if the voice on the other end of the line is practiced in concealing what facial expressions and body language reveal.

Physical Actions: Telemarketers cannot fill out order blanks and hand them to prospects with a pen; yet this is a traditional way to close a face-to-face sale. If prospects worry about a product's com-plexity, telemarketers can arrange a later demonstration to prove it is user-friendly, but they cannot demonstrate on the spot.

Making Adjustments: In telemarketing, everything necessary to a successful transaction depends on the ear and the tongue; the eye and hand are out of the picture. Good telemarketers are exceptional listeners. Deprived of visual cues, they concentrate on catching au-ditory cues. Instead of parroting a script, they make the conversa-tion interactive and listen for a change in tone, a brief pause, or a question that stops in mid-sentence—all indications that something important is happening on the prospect's end.

Knowing prospects also rely heavily on hearing, telemarketers think about their own voices. How they sound can be just as important as what they say since many objections translate into a question of trust. A caller can't rely on a firm handshake and a warm smile to establish trust, but he can put a smile in his voice and talk in the same mode as the prospect. We recommend a mirror on every caller's desk, so he or she check for a smile before beginning each call. Believe it or not, prospects can tell if callers are not smiling.

It's no secret that people like to buy from people just like them. In face-to-face sales, "dressing like the client" is an established principle in some industries. Since a telemarketing prospect can't see who's calling, the caller must establish this bond using only the voice. If the prospect is a deliberate, contemplative person while the caller talks like a horse race announcer, the prospect may miss key points or conclude the caller is a silver-tongued rogue. If the prospect is an energetic, rapid thinker but the caller plods along, measuring every word, the prospect may conclude she is speaking to a slow-witted time-waster. While it may seem like a minor point, training the staff to listen for voice cues and get on the same wavelength as a prospect will pay big dividends.

HARD SELL
VERSUS SOFT SELL

Sources of Pressure: Because telephone contacts are inherently faster than face-to-face contacts, because callers do not have to face disgruntled prospects personally, and because misguided managers create intense pressure, many telephone campaigns are structured on "hard selling." This practice generates several unfortunate results. When jobs hinge on the volume of closings, the ratio of sales to calls made, or the dollar value of sales, anxieties are created that affect the way phoners come across to prospects. Company image = tense.

When a manager is up-tight about results, he or she is likely to seek or tolerate short cuts in sales efforts, and the next tactics callers resort to are chicanery and argument—both death to a legitimate long-term marketing program. Company image = deceitful.

Whenever a campaign develops undesirable overtones of any sort, the impression callers give is amateurish.

In lasting marketing projects "soft sell" approaches are not just desirable, they can make the difference between success and failure.

Distinguishing Hard from Soft: The basic difference between "hard sell" and "soft sell" is in the approach to objections. In the hard sell approach the caller tries to "isolate" the prospect's objection, clearly defining the objection and separating it from the prospect's positive beliefs about the subject. The seller gets the prospect to agree to a sale if the objection is met, then shows the objection is invalid or shows a way around it.

> "Sorry, but I've spent my budget for the year."

> "In other words, Mr. Smith, you liked the features of the product and you can see the benefits to your company, so that if you could budget for this purchase you would order today? Right?"

> "I guess so."

> "Good news, Mr. Smith. We offer extended terms up to 90 days net. That way you can budget for it next quarter and can resell the product and have the cash in hand before you have to pay our invoice. Fifty boxes sounds right for the first order, doesn't it?"

In the soft sell approach, sellers welcome objections as an indication of prospect interest and as an opportunity to provide more information. The seller openly recognizes that the prospect has a legitimate concern, then looks for a solution which addresses the needs on both sides.

> "Sorry, but I've spent my budget for the year."

> "You've got a point. Our company expected some clients would have all their resources committed by this time in the year. That's why we offer several alternate financing arrangements—so you won't miss the biggest promotion of the year."

Objections are rarely overcome by trying to outwit the prospect. The usual result is winning the argument and losing the sale. Even experienced sales people need to be reminded of this if they begin to develop a cocky, arrogant attitude.

The Lure of Hard Sell Tactics: One reason many experienced telemarketers favor isolating and knocking down objections is simplicity. In general, the reasons people give for not wanting to transact business are repetitive (thus, predictable) over a long campaign in which thousands of prospects are contacted.

Consider these easily recognized objections:

1. I don't have time to discuss this.

2. What you're telling me is interesting, but I have to discuss it with my partners (my wife, our sales staff, or any number of other people).

3. I tried that once and it didn't work.

4. It costs too much.

5. I've spent my budget for the year already.

6. I'm not interested.

7. I never buy anything over the telephone.

8. I'm in the process of selling my business.

9. I get your product or service from another supplier, and I'm satisfied.

10. I buy from salesmen who travel to our city. Why are you trying to sell to me over the phone?

11. Your product or service wouldn't benefit us.

12. We're taking Chapter 11 or Chapter 13 bankruptcy.

13. You're talking to the wrong person. I'm not responsible for purchasing your product or service. I can't tell you who handles this.

14. How do I know this isn't a scam?

15. We've been in business 50 years, and we know what we're
    doing. We already have the suppliers we want to do business
    with, and all the customers we could ever want.

Particular industries and consumer markets have their own oft-
repeated objections:

> (Home Improvements) We don't know how long we will
> stay in this house.

> (Advertising) We just depend on word of mouth.

Because these objections are predictable, it is easy to work up
time-tested comebacks. Besting the prospect's argument is fairly
easy since the telemarketer has heard the objection far more often
than the prospect has heard the comeback. (But the objective is
winning the sale, not winning the argument).

Quite often, these objections are simply excuses given by people
who don't want to say no. Because excuses present a challenge,
telemarketers are tempted to resort to the kinds of objection isolating tactics that create ill will. No-win arguments can turn possible
long-range customers into Class D prospects who will never do
business with the caller or the company. To illustrate, let's return to
the hard sell example.

The prospect, having heard the basic offer, says:

> "Sorry, but I've spent my budget for the year."

The phone sales representative tries isolating the objection:

> "In other words, Mr. Smith, you liked the features of the
> product and you can see the benefits to your company, so
> that if you could budget for this purchase you would
> order today? Right?"

Although many telemarketers gloat over this tactic, notice the
prospect's dilemma. Prospects who have the budget objection met
by having words put into their mouths are in an awkward position.
If they say, "Yes, you're right, I do like the product," they know
they have positioned themselves for a sales pitch they don't want to
hear. If instead they say: "But I'm not really interested," they feel

that they may be perceived as having lied in the first place. They are now uncomfortable prospects, either way. So, although the phone representatives may be winning these arguments, they're probably losing sales and damaging relationships with potential long-term customers.

Let's look at the alternative. After hearing the budget objection, the telemarketer responds:

> "You've got a point. Our company expected some clients would have all their resources committed by this time in the year."

This statement demonstrates that the seller understands the prospect's position, which in turn establishes agreement on that much of the selling/purchasing issue. It also opens the way for placing a doubt that the only approach is to wait for a new budget.

> "That's why we offer several alternate financing arrangements—so you won't miss the biggest promotion of the year."

In a subtle way the telemarketer can also remind the prospect that a delay could mean a lost opportunity.

> "We know a few of your competitors may be losing out because they won't be able to make even a test introduction of our product this year for budget reasons."

The telemarketer keeps providing information without trying to take control of the prospect's purchasing decision. Because the prospect feels in control, he is willing to consider the possibilities.

> "What kind of alternative financing are we talking about?"

At this point telemarketers need flexibility. (And managers need to hire people who can handle responsibility.) With a consumer product that can be purchased in varying quantities by a wholesaler, a typical offer might be to send a small test order of about 1/4 the normal initial shipment. This kind of offer should be based on C.O.D. delivery at first. The prospect should be told that if he can turn the initial small inventory quickly, he will be in a better position to make a budget adjustment to accommodate the remainder of what would be a normal initial order.

If the prospect says he can't handle C.O.D. at this time, the caller still has an option.

> "As you perhaps know, our normal terms are a 4% discount for payment within 10 days or no interest for payment within 30 days. I can drop the C.O.D. and give you the same terms, only with 90 days free financing rather than 30. Since yours is a short order that should turn over in one-fourth the normal time, you should have a positive cash flow all the way."

Because the telemarketer has been working to help the prospect solve one of his problems, the prospect shows no resentment when the telemarketer tries to close the deal.

> "Would you consider that a fair enough offer so that we can do a little business now?"

If at this point the prospect still says he can't afford it, the caller will ask when a follow-up call will be appropriate.

MEETING TYPICAL OBJECTIONS

Inexperienced staffers will need help in understanding how to respond to the typical objections listed earlier in this section.

1. I don't have time to discuss this.

   Make an appointment for a better time. If the prospect resists, offer to send a mailing.

2. What you're telling me is interesting, but I have to discuss it with my partners (my wife, my partner's wives, our sales staff, or any number of other people).

   Ask for a good time to call back. Offer to speak to the other decision-maker(s).

3. I tried that once and it didn't work.

   Ask for details. Even if this sale falls through, the information is valuable for marketing.

4. It costs too much.

   Stress value and quality. Find out who the competition is. Consider a limited-time discount to match the competition.

5. I've spent my budget for the year already.
   Present options like those above.

6. I'm not interested.

   Find out why. Can we modify the campaign, product, or support?

7. I never buy anything over the telephone.

   Explain the benefits: talking at convenient times, more personal service, more flexibility, lower costs passed through. Offer mailings and references to increase trust.

8. I'm in the process of selling my business.

   Find out who the prospective owners are and contact them. In the meantime do the current owners need additional stock to keep operating?

9. I get your product or service from another supplier, and I'm satisfied.

   Find out all you can about this arrangement (marketing info). Without attacking the competition, point out your advantages.

10. I buy from salesmen who travel to our city. Why are you trying to sell to me over the phone?

    See answers to number 7.

11. Your product wouldn't benefit us.

    Find out why. They may be right, in which case we need to adjust the campaign, or they may not realize all the benefits of the product.

12. We're taking Chapter 11 (or Chapter 13) bankruptcy.

    Express regrets. If the company will keep operating, ask if they are interested in a C.O.D. shipment. Otherwise, mark the record as a Class D prospect and check back after reorganization.

13. You're talking to the wrong person. I'm not responsible for purchasing your product or service. I can't tell you who handles this.

    Ask the receptionist to help you find the right office.

14. How do I know this isn't a scam?

    Suggest a call to the Better Business Bureau. Send a mailing with references and call back.

15. We've been in business 50 years, and we know what we're doing. We already have the suppliers we want to do business with and all the customers we could ever want.

    Compliment them on their staying power. Ask questions about their operation. Look for unsolved needs.

CLOSING
SIGNALS

An objection which is successfully met opens the door to closing the sale. So do intelligent questions. If the prospect asks for information, it almost always indicates interest. Every telemarketer at Sweet

Caress Candy should be primed to ask for the order after hearing one of these signals:

1. If I give you an order now, how much do I save? Or, What is my total markup?
2. How do you ship them?
3. How much space will a display take in my store?
4. Did you say there are no financing charges?
5. What other stores in my area are carrying your product?
6. Can I return the candy if it doesn't sell?
7. You said the sales forecast in my trade area is $100,000 volume in the first month. Is there a quota that would limit my orders if I find that your candy is a big seller?
8. Are these individually wrapped candies?
9. What is my projected share of the market in a successful campaign?

Each of these statements is a clear indication the prospect is considering a purchase, so a smart telemarketer will ask for a decision.

CLOSING
THE SALE

The Direct Close: The easiest way to make a sale is often the simple direct close: "May I take your order on that basis?" Some prospects will not purchase, but they have no reason to be offended by the approach. If the prospect answers, "No," the caller can easily backtrack: "On what point are you not satisfied?"

The Assumptive Close: Also known as the "Yes-Yes Close" or "Shall I wrap it, or would you like to wear it?" this approach gets mixed reviews. In concept, the technique sounds effective. The telemarketer assumes the sale is made and only asks the prospect to confirm it by making some minor administrative decisions:

"Do we need a purchase order number?"

"Is Thursday good for delivery?"

"Do you need three gross, or will two be enough?"

If the prospect is truly interested, the assumptive close is a smooth efficient way to settle details and nail down the sale. If the prospect is not interested, it is another story.

Perhaps the weakest feature of the assumptive close is the dilemma presented when the answer is "no." The prospect resents being pressured, but the telemarketer has made it difficult for him to say "no." As a result, the "no" that finally comes is emphatic and cold. The door is not only closed; it is padlocked. The prospect cannot retreat from his position without losing face.

Using an assumptive close when it is not appropriate is a good way to eliminate future sales. Never use this method unless the prospect has given a clear signal he intends to buy.

OTHER COMMON
CLOSING METHODS

The direct close and the assumptive close (when used correctly) will always serve the needs of a telemarketing staff. However, since some sales people are more interested in hunting magic formulas than in building relationships, we will discuss some of the fancier closings which may tempt your staff.

The Fear Close: This one is a stock in trade of used car lots. "I know you would like to think it over, but I have another couple coming in half an hour and they are very serious about the car." Telemarketers can also play on fears everyone has to varying degrees at one time or another. If this tactic works, it takes away the prospect's feeling of being in control. To regain control, the prospect is likely to shake off the intimidation and use a hard, cold "no" as an ego defense.

The Hooker Close: The seller drops one hook, and if it does not snag the fish, he drops another.

"If you'll buy a half-carload of detergents for your restrooms today, I'll throw in a half year's supply of paper towels."

Pause and no response.

"That's not all, we'll pick up the shipping costs."

Pause and no response.

"And just in case you think we're not serious, we'll purchase a $200 gift certificate at your favorite clothing store so that you can get our gift of a new suit. How does that sound?"

This approach can generate suspicion. The business owner may wonder why the caller did not mention the best offer at the beginning. Will she have to play cat and mouse to get good terms on future offers? Also, how will she know her competitors are not getting a better break? Finally, what's the deal with the suit? It's legal, but it sounds like some kind of bribe.

Ironically, the prospect may place an initial offer despite her suspicions. She reasons this offer is too good to pass up, but she will not order again unless each pitch is accompanied by another once-in-a-lifetime offer.

There is nothing wrong with offering extras as long as they have some connection with the product. But the extras should be offered up front as part of a package deal. Don't tease the customers!

The Try-It-Out Close: Some telemarketing managers advise their callers to sell on consignment anything which cannot be sold outright.

"Try it on consignment. You have the privilege of returning it at our expense after 10 days, but I'm so sure you'll like it that I'm not worried about getting it back."

This approach will not irritate prospects, and it does close sales, but at a risk. With a well-tested product and honorable customers, this approach will increase sales with minimal effect on returns. Unfortunately, customer motives are sometimes less than honorable. Since auto insurance companies sometimes commit themselves to a policy with the first payment due in 30 days, some customers switch companies every month and pay no premiums.

If you sell a letter-stuffing machine on consignment, a business can use it for their once a year mass mailing and then send it back, thus saving the cost of a rental.

Moral: Use this closing prudently.

The Bandwagon Close: "Everyone else is doing it" has less appeal than it once did. Buyers are more sophisticated, so the appeal must be subtle if it is to work.

"Our schedule is getting very busy, but we can still complete the installation in a week if you order now."

Although the caller quoted above is trying to close a sale, he or she is still presenting valid information to let the prospect make an informed decision without coercion. In the next example the tactic is less subtle.

"If you flip through a recent issue, you can see how many competitors are placing ads with us."

That example is borderline, but the next is over the line.

"We already have most of our distributors lined up. I can't guarantee a quota unless you sign on today."

Whenever the caller puts on pressure to wrest the decision from the prospect, the result is resentment—not a propitious element in a long-term business relationship.

KNOW WHEN TO STOP

When a telemarketer has provided all the necessary information and put the decision squarely in the prospect's lap, that's the time to stop talking. Let the prospect deliberate in silence. People with limited sales experience sometimes have trouble with this concept and may need to be trained not to wreck closings with ill-timed comments. In traditional sales lingo: "Don't talk past the close!"

THE SECRET
TO CLOSING

The best closings develop because the phone representative has effectively taken the role of friend, professional counselor, and customer advocate. At that level of selling, it is easy to lose track of all the techniques that a phone representative uses too close sales. They just seem to close naturally.

KEY POINTS

1. Many of the visual cues which signal a client is ready to close are not available over the phone. Consequently, telemarketers must listen carefully, not only for words, but also for pauses and tone of voice.

2. Telemarketers should pay attention to their own voices to make sure they sound friendly and trustworthy and to make adjustments to match the prospect's rate of speech.

3. The basic difference between hard sell and soft sell tactics is in the approach to objections. In the preferred soft sell approach, the seller recognizes the prospect has a legitimate concern, then looks for a solution which addresses the needs on both sides.

4. A hard sell approach which isolates and invalidates each objection leaves the prospect feeling resentful and no longer in control of the buying decision.

5. An objection which is met or an intelligent question about the product signals the telemarketer to try closing the sale.

7. The simplest closing is direct: "May I take your order on that basis?"

8. The assumptive close, in which the seller assumes the deal is done and simply asks about details, will backfire if the prospect has not decided to buy.

9. The best closings are the most natural.

CHAPTER 10

HOW TO BUILD A WINNING TEAM

The best strategy is no better than the team which must implement it. Nowhere is this dictum truer than in telemarketing. Look at any floundering telemarketing program, and (no matter what else is wrong) you will usually find a staff which is ill-equipped for the job. Fortunately, the antidote is not hard to find. As we have said before, the answer is to hire well, train well, and pay well.

THE OUTSIDE ALTERNATIVE

If your company does not already have a telemarketing staff, you may want to weigh the pros and cons of hiring an outside contractor instead of setting up an in-house program. For more information on this option, consult Appendix 2.

To learn more about building a team within the company, read on.

JOB REQUIREMENTS

Good telemarketers can be found inside or outside the company, but only if you know what to look for. To be successful, telemarketers need the traits listed below; whether they gain them from training or have them when hired.

Desired Voice Traits: A telemarketer needs to sound pleasant and trustworthy, be easily understood, be enthusiastic, and have a voice people like to hear. Good telephone voices come in many variations, but you don't want to hire someone who mumbles, has a heavy accent, has a whiny voice, puts people to sleep with a monotone, or has a high-pitched voice that grates on the nerves.

Desired Personality Traits: Everyone in the operation needs to be basically friendly and interested in helping others. The operation will also run better if the people in it like each other and work well together.

Telemarketers should also be confident in their abilities, but not arrogant. They should have an ability to handle rejection and operate under pressure without getting defensive.

Listening Skills: A glib talker who never listens has a severe handicap in marketing. Search for people who not only pause to listen but also have the ability to empathize, read between the lines, and analyze what they hear.

Writing Ability: We have discussed the advantages of having telemarketers write their own letters. That's only possible if they write well.

Product Knowledge: Telemarketers don't need to know as much as the design staff, but they will have to handle routine customer questions.

Work Preferences: This one seems self-evident, but sometimes managers ignore the obvious. To be successful a telemarketer must spend long hours sitting and talking in a small room. People who do not like those conditions will be unhappy. Some prospective staff members would rather travel, or work outside, or work with their hands, or *see* who they talk with, or have a change of scenery by visiting other offices each day. Hire someone who would rather sit and talk.

Experience: The best possible background includes knowledge of the product and experience in a quality telemarketing program. An applicant with a boiler-room background must be able to overcome it by changing philosophy as well as habits. Even people who have never worked in telephone sales may have misconceptions which lead to pressure tactics. People who get a lot of hard-sell calls at home may assume that is the only way to sell.

Do Disabilities Matter? Paraplegics are successful telemarketers; so are victims of severe burns or cerebral palsy. In fact, some telemarketing firms only hire handicapped workers. In operations where seller and prospect never meet, the most severe disfigurement is no handicap. Even the physical requirements are very simple: a job candidate must have a good voice and be able to manipulate the telephone equipment and the record-keeping system. When we consider the range of equipment now available to help handicapped people operate telephone equipment and the sophisticated services which can link home and office, only a handful of people are physically unqualified as telemarketers.

STRUCTURING
THE JOB

Some of the questions we have raised in other chapters need to be resolved before employee selection begins.

Defining the Scope: Will the job be full-time or part-time, or will it be an additional responsibility tacked on to another job? Simply adding telemarketing to the job description of another position looks attractive, but that path is strewn with obstacles. Giving telemarketing responsibility to an employee who is already feeling overworked will guarantee resentment. The employee will cut corners somewhere, by letting other responsibilities slip, by not making the telemarketing calls, or by making them perfunctorily.

Adding a small telemarketing operation without adding positions is possible, but it requires careful analysis before acting. If some other factor (declining sales, perhaps) is decreasing the workload in various positions, the manager may be able to shuffle job responsibilities and get telemarketing into the hands of someone with the time and talent to do it well.

If the combined workload does not have enough slack for that approach and the telemarketing responsibility is still less than a full-time job the manager has two options:

1. Hire part-time help.

2. Hire full-time, but combine telemarketing with other responsibilities. The new telemarketer could also handle purchasing, for instance.

Combining telemarketing with other responsibilities has both advantages and disadvantages. The strain of having to be "up" for every call begins to wear on most telemarketers after a few hours. Being able to switch to other duties can lessen the strain and make individual calls more effective. On the downside, being able to switch to other duties allows an escape from the various unpleasantries associated with cold calling. A telemarketer/bookkeeper may end up keeping immaculate books and making almost no phone calls.

A manager who is alert for this problem has several options. She can opt for a technological fix and buy some form of "call accounting," which will furnish a printed record of every call. Or, she can elect a simpler solution, if the job responsibilities allow it, by setting firm time limits for each part of the job—only telemarketing in the morning, only bookkeeping in the afternoon.

Defining the Duties: Will the operation be divided between lead finders and closers? If so, the lead finders will not need as much product knowledge.

Will the position require writing letters? If so, writing skills should be evaluated during the hiring process.

The more exactly you can define the telemarketer's duties, the easier it becomes to evaluate job candidates.

SOURCES FOR
NEW STAFF

The manager putting together a team has basically two choices: recruit from inside the company or hire from outside.

Inside Sources: Anyone on the payroll who is articulate and has the required skills and personality traits is a possible candidate, but be careful about assuming too much. Insiders may need re-education just as much as outsiders; long-term employees may not realize telemarketing involves long hours behind a desk, may expect to use boiler-room tactics, may possess surprisingly little knowledge about the product, or may expect a demeaning, underpaid job. Well-designed job announcements and bulletin board notices which explain what the job is really like can dispel these myths.

Certain areas in the organization are more likely hunting grounds:

—Employees charged with product maintenance are likely to have strong product knowledge.

—The over-the-counter sales staff have sales experience and a feel for customer concerns.

—Receptionists, secretaries, and order-takers are usually experienced on the telephone.

—Customer service representatives are likely to know the customers and the product.

—The outside sales force has sales experience, product knowledge, and insight into customer preferences, but they may have a determined antipathy toward telemarketing.

Outside Sources: Consider all the usual methods for finding employees, such as informal networking, job placement agencies, and advertising. You may need to be fairly specific in explaining that the job involves interactive telemarketing. Otherwise, you will have to weed out the boiler-room retreads. A typical classified ad would read:

> "A manufacturer of candies and confections has an open-ing for a telemarketing account manager. Duties involve maintaining service to old clients by letters and phone calls and prospecting for new clients by calling to ask questions and discuss the prospect's needs. Salary and commission negotiable based on experience. Full benefits. Call 789-0123."

The last sentence in this ad is a little unusual. Rather than asking for resumes, we prefer asking for a phone call. Resumes are a poor screening device for this job because they do not reveal telephone personalities. When the calls come in, the interviewer can ask each candidate to describe his or her background. Because people gener-ally expect to be hired on the basis of a resume and face-to-face interview, they rarely put on a front during the initial phone call. Thus, the interviewer can experience each candidate's voice and personality exactly as a prospect would. A candidate who survives this initial screening would bring a resume to a face-to-face inter-view.

INITIAL TRAINING

Sources: A company can do its own training using internal re-sources or hire another firm to perform the training.

Using internal resources lessens the out-of-pocket expenses and ensures the program will be tailored to the company's needs. It does require a considerable amount of planning, a knowledge of training principles, and some experience in the field. If the manager and staff are all inexperienced in telemarketing, we would recom-mend another option.

Hiring someone to come in and train the staff simplifies the pro-cess, but increases the cost. Outside trainers typically bring with them a wealth of experience plus a solid grounding in training techniques. If you choose this option, make sure the outside trainer(s) understand your market and your product. Product experts from within the company may need to handle the sessions on product knowledge.

Designing the Course: The staff's background will dictate which elements need to be stressed in a training program. A recycled traveling salesman will not need to be told much about assumptive closes, but he may have trouble recognizing the opportunity to use one when deprived of his familiar visual cues. An experienced telemarketer hired from outside may be great at listening for cues but weak in product knowledge.

Whatever the staff's background, we recommend starting with a solid grounding in telemarketing concepts and the philosophy of this particular program. One means to that end which does not take a lot of the trainer's time is to have everyone read a short book on the subject and discuss the key concepts. *(Teleselling* by Philip E. Mahfood is one possibility.) To ensure everyone reads the book, ask them to supply written answers to a couple of key questions from each chapter.

When the staff is in agreement on basic operating principles, bring in product knowledge. In addition to briefings from design engineers and service personnel, consider required reading assignments from catalogs, service manuals, spec sheets, and the like. Ask the trainees to develop the tools they will need: lists of facts, benefits, and typical questions. (See Chapter Three.)

Ask the more experienced trainees to demonstrate effective courteous responses to typical objections; then move into role-playing. This is not just a demonstration. Every trainee should get to handle each of the typical prospect responses. We strongly advocate using maximum simulation. If only a few people are in training, have each one sit at his or her desk with the appropriate poop sheets and a calling list handy. Each call goes to another extension where the trainer sits. The calls get progressively tougher as the trainer assumes a variety of roles.

With a large number of trainees, a simple one-on-one role-play is difficult if everyone is involved. One technique we have used successfully in a large class is to divide everyone into groups of three. Each trio includes a caller, a prospect, and an observer. Each trio arranges their positions so the caller and prospect can hear but not see each other. They may sit side by side but face straight ahead or the caller may sit while the prospect stands behind him or her. The caller is equipped with the usual poop sheets and calling list; the prospect has a stack of index cards with instructions. The first card might read:

> "On call one you are a person determined never to buy anything over the phone. Last year you purchased two skids of defective garden edging from an out-of-state supplier and were never able to get your money back."

The caller in this scenario must recognize this impasse and work around it. The observer, who is equipped with a checklist, watches the action and critiques the caller at the end.

The final step in a good training program is coaching. The trainer silently monitors actual cold calls and debriefs the caller after each call. As with any other type of training, a critical element in equipping ordinary people to become powerful telemarketers is attitude. Talk about what you want to happen, not what you fear will happen.

In a job where rejection is inevitable, the biggest key to success is a positive, supportive environment.

KEY POINTS

1. Whether a company promotes from within or hires from outside, prospective telemarketers need to be friendly, have good voices, listen and write well, know the product, and enjoy sitting at a desk talking on the phone.

2. Disabilities do not disqualify a job candidate so long as he or she can talk clearly and operate the equipment.

3. Management must decide at the outset whether to hire full-time, hire part-time, or combine telemarketing with some other job.

4. If an employee does telemarketing combined with another job, the manager must ensure the less pleasant telemarketing functions are also completed.

5. Whether the company seeks to hire from inside or outside, the job description must distinguish this operation from the boiler-room stereotype.

6. The first interview with a job candidate should be by phone.

7. A good training program will cover the basic principles of telemarketing, the philosophy of the particular program, the essentials of product knowledge, and methods for handling objections and closings. It will conclude with intensive role-plays followed by real calls monitored by the trainer.

CHAPTER 11

BURNOUT PREVENTION AND TREATMENT

THE CONDITION

The term "job burnout" is bandied about in the workplace so often it is not always taken seriously. In some groups the term has come to mean any sort of unpleasant sensation. Thus, "I'm burned out," might be translated as, "I'm feeling out of sorts," or "I'm a little hung over." But real job burnout, which can enervate and immobilize good workers, is a serious problem. Unfortunately, it is also an occupational hazard for telemarketers.

Serious burnout is a form of depression. While it can be aggravated by the classical causes of depression (such as family conflicts, loss of self-esteem, and the like) job burnout derives from job-related problems. The condition is a particular problem for telemarketers because activities like cold calling require an upbeat positive attitude. Without confidence, people can't pick up the phone and make calls. So a little bit of depression goes a long way toward paralyzing an operation.

By definition, job burnout is a job-threatening condition. As a result, victims and their colleagues may deny there is a problem and sweep it under the carpet until the carpet is so out of shape they trip and fall. To keep the operation running smoothly, managers need to be alert for burnout symptoms. A victim typically feels

161

out of control, with too much pressure on the job and too little goal achievement. A person who was very positive may start making ambivalent statements about the job and may complain of disturbed sleep, general anxiety, lack of concentration, muscle pain, or any other of the common stress-related ailments.

Ultimately, the condition can be so debilitating a person starts missing work or comes in and only stares at the phone.

PREVENTION

Effective burnout prevention strategies involve both managers and staff. If telemarketers have been trained to recognize incipient burnout and think calmly about their problems at work, they can frequently nip the problem in the bud. Managers can help by encouraging callers to stay alert for the problem, enlisting group support, and keeping an open environment for discussion.

Mutual Support: Management can encourage the staff to function as a guided support group—to lend encouragement to those who are having a rough day or a rough week. This approach will not work if the group loses sight of its purpose. Trading gripes around the coffee machine is not lending support and may send people back to work even more frustrated.

Open Atmosphere: Managers can help by encouraging callers to talk freely and comfortably about what bothers them. Even if the manager's policies are causing the frustration, employees should be able to air their concerns without fear of retribution. Often the problem cannot be solved, but talking about it can ease some of the pain that is blocking productive work.

CAUSES AND
TREATMENT

When formerly productive workers start staring at the phone, it usually is a sign something has changed. Finding the cause and coping with it can sometimes get the worker back on track. While the following list is not exhaustive, it shows some of the most likely places for trouble.

1. A new supervisor. The caller has to cope with new procedures and new pressures. If, in fact, this is the problem, the supervisor cannot afford to be thin-skinned. Employees are frequently in the best position to know what works and what doesn't; ignoring their inputs will hasten burnout and increase turnover.

2. A new tight script. The caller feels he has lost control over his activities; he has to say things that don't work. This problem could have been prevented by involving the callers in designing the program. Failing that, a mid-course correction is definitely in order.

3. A losing streak. The same approach that worked until recently is not working at all. Nobody is buying from this caller. Top managers can dampen panic by telling about their own bad streaks and others they know about. Every campaign has its good and bad periods. If the marketing information from unsuccessful calls indicates the campaign is still on track, there is no reason to panic.

4. No enthusiasm. Every approach eventually gets boring. Management should encourage callers to experiment by trying a different opening or looking for other benefits. Getting a caller to focus on improving the pattern can usually rekindle interest. A couple of days off can have the same effect.

5. Rotten prospects. People are starting to get to the caller. This is a good time to assign some administrative duties without prejudice and take the caller off the phone for a few days or a few weeks. The manager can even delegate some of her responsibilities to broaden the caller's perspective.

6. Loss of faith in the product. If the production line is close, arrange for the caller to have a tour. Ask the production manager to focus on quality control, application of sophisticated

machinery and methods, and morale. For loss of faith in the product's benefits, arrange a tour of a satisfied customer's site.

7. Late commissions. The true cause of late commissions may be slow collections. The manager and caller should review delinquent accounts with the accounting department. With a little training, the caller can also be enlisted to collect from his or her accounts.

8. Intense competition. The department hotshot may be bragging about his sales, causing representatives with smaller, slower accounts to worry about their jobs. The boss can reassure the worried callers and ask the hotshot to cool it. This kind of problem can be caused by policies which favor individual instead of group competition. If every member of the group gets a modest reward when the group meets its goals, members are likelier to help and encourage each other.

9. Economic downturn. The staff is growing restive because a recession has lowered sales, commissions, and expectations. Unpaid bills are a worry. Management can't do much with this problem except to help representatives ride it out by offering advances against commissions or helping them find salary work within the company.

The manager's role in curing burnout really goes beyond these specific suggestions. A good supervisor or manager will be consistently aware of the individual telemarketers' needs and search for ways to meet them—just as the individual callers seek to meet the customers' needs.

SELF-INFLICTED BURNS

Telemarketers can create their own burnout by poor work habits: missing callbacks because of poor organization, failing to mail follow-up letters because of poor time management, asking dumb questions because of poor record-keeping. Eventually the telemarketer gets overwhelmed by his own incompetence. Managers can help cure these self-inflicted burns by careful coaching, designed to substitute better work habits while raising confidence levels.

MANAGEMENT ACTIONS

Preventing burnout is more than just reacting when callers develop the symptoms. A company can build burnout prevention into its planning with actions such as these.

1. Hire tough and resilient people. Ask candidates how they handle rejection and how they handle change. Ask them to tell you about a defeat and how they recovered from it.

2. Keep repeating that marketing information is vital. A no-sale phone call is not a failure if the caller can bring back important information.

3. Give the staff control over their functions by letting them participate in planning each new marketing campaign.

4. Treat the telemarketers as important people. Spend the money to give them comfortable working conditions and good equipment.

5. Don't set impossible goals. Rumplestiltskin could turn straw into gold, but telemarketing is no fairy tale. The telemarketing manager should test every new program by making the initial calls personally and keeping statistics. Keeping those statistics as a benchmark will ensure telemarketers are not asked to do the impossible.

6. Train telemarketers to be professional in discussions with each other about how well or poorly they are doing. A good department has no room for one-upsmanship or pity parties. The group needs to be mutually supportive and help each other realistically deal with problems.

7. Encourage callers to take frequent breaks as long as they don't abuse the privilege or use the breaks to spread gloom. Phone

work is intense. To keep maximum concentration, people need to relax frequently. A liberal break policy can even be presented as one of the perks of a tough job.

8. Make it worthwhile to stay through the tough times. In other words, put something in the compensation package to encourage longevity. A good retirement package is not enough. Today's eager young workers won't wait that long. Consider incentives spaced every two or three years.

9. Make open communications a company policy. Every member of the telemarketing staff should be able to discuss sales problems without fearing they will be slighted for being honest.

10. Make sure your product or service matches the promises you want telemarketers to make.

11. Consider hiring a professional consultant for serious burnout problems. Increased productivity should more than cover the fee.

THE KEY INGREDIENT

Whatever approach you take in attacking burnout, never forget sensitivity. Human beings do not want to work for robots; they want to work for people who care about what happens to them.

If people are the most important resource, preserving that resource is the most important management function.

KEY POINTS

1. Job burnout, a form of depression, is a serious problem in telemarketing; burnout can immobilize formerly effective staff members.

2. Effective burnout prevention involves both managers and staff.

3. Managers should encourage callers to talk freely about what bothers them without fear of retribution and should help callers support each other.

4. Particular causes of burnout, such as loss of faith in the product, have particular remedies in addition to general support and openness.

5. A company should include burnout prevention in its planning with actions such as these:

   a. Hiring tough and resilient people.

   b. Letting everyone know that a no-sale phone call is not a failure if it yields valid marketing information.

   c. Using callers to help plan each new campaign.

   d. Providing good equipment and good working conditions.

   e. Setting realistic goals based on calls made by the telemarketing manager in the test phase of the program.

   f. Training telemarketers to be professional in talking about their work—no one-upsmanship or pity parties.

   g. Encouraging frequent breaks.

   h. Structuring the compensation package to encourage longevity.

   i. Having a policy of *not* shooting the messenger.

   j. Hiring a professional consultant for serious burnout problems.

   k. Making sure the product matches the promises.

CHAPTER 12

BURNOUT REMEDIES: A CASE STUDY

TYPICAL EXCUSES

Turnover in telephone sales rooms is often taken for granted. Some managers seem to feel the telephone, itself, is a valid excuse for attrition. They may justify high turnover by assuming the low cost of phone calls and mail in relation to travel more than compensates for the expense of continually training new personnel. However, they fail to consider the hidden costs of lost sales and defecting customers—both likely results with an inexperienced staff.

At the lower depths of the industry, boiler-room bosses jack up sales with a combination of flashy incentives and draconian pressure, consciously sacrificing longevity for fast profits. The results can be bizarre. One manager bragged to one of us that he could stand outside the boiler-room door and judge the efficiency of his callers by the decibel level. In other companies, unreasonable sales quotas guarantee the only people around for years will be men and women with permanently maladjusted personalities.

In other cases a boss pays minuscules wages but feeds young egos by staging delirious victory demonstrations and conferring bragging rights when a sale is made.

These examples are extremes. Even a company that wants to operate a normal telephone marketing and sales department can encounter problems that create frustrations leading to burnout.

THE CASE HISTORY

Turnover: In this case a medical supply company—let's call it Aerobic Mediquip—discovered the telemarketing department was struggling with an annual turnover of 90%, for reasons not immediately apparent.

Personnel records revealed the average period of effective phone selling ranged between six and nine months. At the point of incapacitation, callers either quit or were fired. Only three people had survived past one year; the senior caller had a tenure of four years. Two others had been with the company for two years.

The instability was particularly distressing for senior management, for the department was selling a line of electrocardiogram machines to small clinics and doctor's offices—exactly the type of market in which long-term relationships are critical.

Another group within the company functioned as an outside sales staff selling hospitals a diverse line of surgical and medical equipment.

Cause: Product Failure: When management interviewed the telemarketing staff, the cause of the burnout problem was discovered. Telemarketers were intensely frustrated and discouraged over their inability to deal with complaints about machine breakdowns. Service records showed 10% of the EKG machines broke down within six months after the doctors purchased them.

Cause: Misguided Recruiting: A contributing factor was the method of recruiting. To keep phones staffed in the face of high turnover, the company kept the local newspapers well supplied with help-wanted ads. Whenever a desk was vacant, the telemarketing manager hired the first person with sales experience who would take the job. Most recruits were traveling sales representatives for a wide variety of products and services who wanted to come off the road for personal reasons. Others were door-to-door canvassers seeking to take a step up; still others were retail sales clerks who were tired of standing on their feet all day. A few were telephone sales people who had job-hopped in and out of many boiler rooms. All were articulate and persuasive.

With few exceptions, the staff members viewed their employment by Aerobic Mediquip as a means of solving personal problems. Typically, the traveling sales representatives who were retiring from the road were looking for the best of both possible worlds—an exciting 9 to 5 selling opportunity and a better home life.

An important attraction for newcomers was the potentially high annual income from sink-or-swim commission levels. When the problem was spotted in the early 1980s, the four-year veteran was earning $100,000 a year, with those who had been on the job two years getting $60,000 and $70,000. In addition, the company offered an excellent health insurance program including dental and eye care insurance, and liberal vacations after the first year. Aerobic Mediquip sweetened its compensation pot with a typical incentive program featuring substantial prizes for telemarketers and their spouses based on general performance and gross sales.

Yet the combination of these values did not overcome the demoralization that resulted from the glitch in customer relations. With 10% of the machines breaking down, sooner or later every staff member had to bear the brunt of angry complaints and had to deal with service problems or returned merchandise.

Dodging the Failure Problem: Even though the telemarketers were advised of the expected breakdown rate and were encouraged to discuss it with buyers at the time of sale, not many did. Instead, they skated past the problem and hoped for the best.

The high cost of the EKG machines ($60,000) meant most of the doctors and clinics could only afford one. When that machine quit and patients had to be sent elsewhere, a typical clinic director became extremely unpleasant. Fielding these complaints demoralized the extroverted sales people Mediquip was hiring. Despite the service department's efforts, some repairs took several days, during which the telemarketer would get an angry call every morning.

Added Rejection: The negative effects of complaints were magnified because normal sales closings ran 1 in 30. Obviously, that meant that for every sale a representative made, he or she had to face an average of 29 rejections. In other operations selling high-profit items, practiced telemarketers have a reasonable tolerance, even for frequent rejections, because they can laugh all the way to the bank. In this case, the combination of frequent rejection and periodic chewing out made the average telemarketer's stay at Mediquip quite short.

Spreading the Bad News: Telemarketers at Mediquip had comfortable private offices, but they were small and clustered, being formed from movable seven-foot high partitions. As a result, when a sales person had a particularly sharp tongue-lashing from an irritated doctor or a nervous lay assistant complaining about failed equipment, the word spread quickly. Other callers became demoralized and dreaded picking up the phone. From the telemarketers' standpoint, every day brought someone a disaster since the angry calls from doctor's offices often meant a total loss of a sale and a commission.

Solutions: the Early Attempts: At one point Mediquip attempted to separate the sales and customer relations functions. One approach was to have the service manager try to field complaints and mollify irate customers. This method failed because, even though the service manager was an authority on repair procedures, the angered customer wanted to be heard by the person who made the sale.

Another approach had customer relations personnel relieve the sales representatives of the complaint handling function, but customers were no happier with customer relations representatives than they were with the service manager, and for the same reason. Customers weren't happy until they could chastise sales representatives for selling them a defective product.

Solution: The Recovery Room Concept: Determined to stop the hemorrhage of talent but bereft of ideas, top management at Mediquip called an outside consultant.

After a brief study of the situation, the consultant recommended setting up a Recovery Room where temporarily dysfunctional telemarketers could comfortably isolate themselves for relaxation and recreation after episodes of phone shock. This area was to be used for the sole purpose of letting wounded callers recover their morale before returning to the phone. The room would not only allow one battered caller to recuperate, it would protect the rest of the staff from another "ain't it awful" story. Thus, one person's discouragement would not spread to everyone else.

The consultant suggested a design incorporating relevant humor, beginning with the sign on the door: "RECOVERY ROOM—FOR USE OF WALKING WOUNDED ONLY." Inside would be a cheerful unisex decor, and some basic recreation equipment: such as a pin-ball machine and a punching bag. A small refrigerator would be stocked with soft drinks and simple, but healthy snacks.

Recovery Room Rules: In order for the room to function as a psychological safety valve, to divert phoners from their troubles and to return them to the telephone cured and cheerful in minimum time, simple ground rules would be needed. The consultant and the telemarketing manager agreed on these:

1. The manager was to utilize the room generously whenever a condition in the phone room called for it.

2. Each telemarketer would report the content of any demoralizing telephone call to the manager as quickly as the call ended.

3. The report of frustration was to be audiotaped for playback and for collection in an archives which could be utilized in internal anti-frustration seminars.

4. Before entering the Recovery Room a caller would have to estimate the time needed away from the phone before he or she would be ready to tackle the next telephone sale. It was understood that the estimate was to serve as a personal con-

tract—the first step in forgetting about the annoying episode and getting on with business.

5. The Recovery Room would be locked when unoccupied and would be used only for recovery by telemarketers.

6. Callers who met their recovery goals ("back to work in two hours") would get a merchandise prize, a get-well gift. The shorter the goal, the higher the prize. Anyone whose recovery goal was over three hours would receive a one dollar booby prize.

7. Although the policy was liberal, use of the room was not automatic. The manager would have to judge the validity of each request.

8. As a curb on abuse, major awards would be given at an annual meeting to those callers who spent the least time in the Recovery Room.

The Recovery Process: Two key concepts made the Recovery Room work. People were encouraged to laugh at situations that were causing distress and they were made to realize they were not alone. The fact that a major company needed a Recovery Room to take care of the victims of telephone stress showed everyone the problem must be fairly common. That meant people in the room were normal and not failures. They therefore felt no need to agonize over the irate customer or their feelings of incompetence.

The need for humor got special attention. Signs on the walls included these examples:

"You're probably saner than you think."

"My mother told me there'd be days like this, but what was she selling on the phone?"

"You think you got troubles—the president of the company spent two weeks in here."

"This is a Recovery Room, not a hospital; don't expect a cute nurse."

"The next person who walks in injured might be your manager"

"If someone else gets here before you leave, you can begin group therapy."

"We don't take temperatures; we just cool tempers."

"When you can laugh at whatever got you here, you've recovered, so leave your get-well gift order at the door."

If we were going to implement the Recovery Room in another organization, we would add sheets of newsprint taped on the walls to invite graffiti.

By chuckling at the situation and losing themselves in a few rounds of pinball (or Nintendo) callers realize things are not as grim as they seemed. They also realize other people are still out there weathering the storms—these situations aren't impossible after all.

If a second sales person arrives before the first one leaves, each knows that the other is suffering similar frustrations. On the basis of incentives set up for early return to phones, they are likely to help each other recover. Thus, a support network gradually forms.

Changing Incentives: Under prodding from the consultant, Mediquip reexamined its sales incentive program. The company had a typically unimaginative incentive program with no proven results. Major prizes based on exceeding quotas included such things as paid vacation trips. For the three senior telemarketers, commission compensation was high and steady; extra prizes did not represent major values. For the rest of the sales force, such prizes were a potential irritant, especially when burnout was setting in. The wife of a newly hired telemarketer might be pushing him to win the Hawaii vacation, which he knew was unattainable. He could not compete successfully against the four-year veteran, and having to compete just added another pressure on top of the problems with angry customers.

Mediquip scrapped this incentive program and in its place adopted a cheaper one. In addition to the get-well gifts to callers who met their recovery contracts, major prizes were given to those who rarely needed to recover, and frequent longevity bonuses were instituted. Although the incentives that were adopted to help prevent burnout might not have been as exciting as the previous ones, they more directly attacked the overriding problem in the telemarketing department.

Although Mediquip did not look at this angle, any company seriously considering revamping its incentive plan should consider an incentive for lowering customer defections. For a variety of reasons, old customers are more valuable than new customers. Some of the extra profit old customers bring in should be spent on programs to retain them. Giving a prize to every caller who keeps old customer defections below a target percentage will be money well spent.

The Team Approach to Complaints: In addition to setting the engineers to work to solve the reliability problem, Mediquip management took another look at the customer service arrangement. They put the customer relations staff back in the line of fire, but with a difference. Customer relations staff were empowered to settle minor complaints directly, but they no longer tried to shelter telemarketers from angry customers.

For more difficult complaints, the customer relations specialist had the option of bringing the service manager and the telemarketing account representative on the line. Everyone with insight on the problem was now available to help in its resolution. Should the account representative not be available when the customer was on the line, the customer relations specialist took down all relevant information and forwarded it to the account representative. Mediquip policy required the account representative to research the problem and get back to the customer within 24 hours.

While this approach does not seem radically different from the earlier solutions, it worked better for several reasons:

1. Because the customer relations staff have the power to solve the simple problems, many complaints never reach the telemarketers—less hassle, less burnout.

2. Having three Mediquip people tackle the tough complaints increases the chance of finding a solution and lessens the like-

lihood of one person being intimidated by a belligerent customer.

3. The process seems logical to customers in the medical profession in which teams of specialists assemble quickly to jointly solve individual health problems.

Mediquip also furnished team members lists of actions to pacify irate customers, that is, suggested alternatives to returning the machine:

1. Use of a "loaner" machine when the customer's unit was not functional. However, these machines were not always available.

2. Paying the doctor's out-of-pocket costs for EKGs done elsewhere because of a breakdown.

3. Giving an "inconvenience discount" based on the number of days a machine was out of service.

Using these tools, teams were able to improve customer satisfaction while lessening telemarketers' burnout.

Improved Recruiting: At the consultant's suggestion, Mediquip tightened its hiring policy and started looking for people with extensive telemarketing experience in high-quality operations. In other words, they began seeking people whose longevity attested to their toughness. These people had faced rejection while selling slow-moving high-ticket items before, had handled angry customers without folding, and had a track record with a low incidence of burnout. Those who were hired adapted rapidly.

Improved Training: Predictably, the company was unable to fill every vacancy with veteran telemarketers. To fill the gap, they began hiring inexperienced, but talented people and sending them to the customer relations department for training. For four to eight weeks each recruit handled customer complaints. While it might seem this approach was a "baptism by fire," actually the pressure was lower in the customer relations department than in the telemarketing department for a very good reason: the customer relations specialist did not have a huge commission at risk when a customer called.

This method showed several advantages:

1. Trainees rapidly picked up technical knowledge of the product's strengths and weaknesses.

2. Trainees learned techniques in negotiation, claims settlement, and listening skills that would prove invaluable in alleviating hostility later.

3. Trainees became skilled in handling the telephone equipment.

4. Trainees became conditioned to the routine of phone work. Those who felt uncomfortable left before switching to the more difficult job.

5. Management had a valid basis for judging each trainee's personality and phone performance in actual practice related closely to future responsibilities. Bad risks could be released before much damage was done.

LESSONS LEARNED

This type of combination strategy can effectively reduce, though rarely eliminate, burnout. The keys to success are ferreting out the true causes in a particular case, using imagination to think of solutions beyond the obvious, and staying flexible.

KEY POINTS

1. A medical equipment company had 90% turnover in its telemarketing department because the callers could not handle the angry complaints from customers.

2. The company lowered the high burnout rate by providing a Recovery Room where callers could relax and recuperate after a rough call. The room provided humor, recreation, and food.

3. Before entering the Recovery Room each caller would set a recovery goal ("back to work in two hours").

4. Callers who met their recovery goals got get-well gifts and those who used the room least got awards at a company meeting.

5. The company also adopted a team approach to customer complaints. A customer relations specialist, the telemarketer who sold the product, and the service manager would all try to help find a solution. This approach lessened the intimidation of telemarketers.

6. The company changed its recruiting to pick up more experienced telemarketers, people who were better able to endure burnout conditions.

7. New inexperienced telemarketers were put to work temporarily in the customer relations department where they learned to handle customers under less stressful conditions than in the telemarketing department.

CHAPTER 13

TELEMARKETING TO FORTUNE 500 COMPANIES: A CASE STUDY

THE CHALLENGE

Selling to the largest corporations in America, those which have made the Fortune 500 list, represents the ultimate challenge in telemarketing. These companies, with their complicated, sometimes Byzantine, buying procedures can be difficult to penetrate.

Because the potential profit from repeated sales is huge, the competition is keen. Sellers of every imaginable product and service are lined up to meet real or imagined needs.

If your company offers a new product serving a recognized need, you can become established rapidly if there's nothing else like it on the market. Such products and services, however, are rare. The average company finds itself competing with a host of competitors, all equally determined and resourceful.

What makes for successful telemarketing at this level is what makes for success at any level in the market—careful planning of both the product and the marketing concept, hard work in executing the plan, and flexibility in allowing for changes along the way. What's different is the level of patience required; big companies don't move as fast as small ones.

CASE HISTORY
BACKGROUND

That need for patience is plainly evident as we follow two partners who hired a small telemarketing firm to launch a new product targeted at America's largest corporations.

Although the principal participants in this program are identified fictitiously, and the names of customers and prospects are withheld for proprietary reasons, the information that follows is accurate and well documented. Of even greater importance, it reveals how a telemarketing program can be developed from scratch in a most complex domestic market, and what it takes to sustain such a program.

Having one of the authors of this book as a character in the drama presented us with a stylistic dilemma. To say, "I consulted with the owners," is awkward when there are two authors. To say, "We consulted," is untrue. We have chosen to escape the dilemma by describing events in the third person.

THE PRINCIPALS

A professor in speech communication at a private university approached Walter Woolfson about marketing a video cassette series on Negotiation and Bargaining Skills.

The professor (let's call him Arthur Fox) had worked with a colleague (Herman Barclay) to develop an award-winning training package—six hour-long video cassettes integrated with five workbooks. The package had taken a bronze medal in the "Videotape of the Year" competition held by the Information Film Producers of America. Fox and Barclay had incorporated under the name "Winning Words."

A management analyst would have said the company had a great product but a serious capital shortage. Because they were sailing in unfamiliar waters, neither man was comfortable with outside financing. They dug into their own pockets to start the company and hoped to finance expansion from the early revenues.

AVAILABLE RESOURCES

To minimize the initial outlay for marketing, they offered Walter Woolfson and Company a commission-only contract. Fox and Barclay believed the package would sell for $600. They offered Woolfson and Company exclusive rights with a 50% gross commission on all sales and control of the marketing effort. In addition to the usual office overhead, Woolfson and Company would absorb the expenses for telephone calls and correspondence.

At first, Woolfson was inclined to refuse the offer because his small staff was fully engaged in other projects and had little time to take on one more project. The lack of capital was also worrisome, but his review of the videotape package showed it to be highly creative and closely matched to demonstrated needs in the workplace.

Ultimately, Woolfson took the offer. Since the staff was engaged in other profitable projects, this one would not have to turn a profit immediately. With full-time jobs, the professors could also afford to be patient, and a slow start would allow time to smooth out the inevitable rough edges. If sales picked up immediately, Woolfson and Company could afford to add staff.

THE FIRST PROMOTION PACKAGE

The telemarketing staff worked with Dr. Fox and Dr. Barclay to create the necessary telemarketing tools (fact, benefit, and question/answer sheets). Woolfson then created a simple follow-up mailing with these components:

1. A customized cover letter reviewing the various applications of the training materials which were given on the phone.

2. A complete workbook.

3. Resumes for Dr. Fox and Dr. Barclay.

4. An order form.

5. A ten-minute demonstration video.

The ten-minute demonstration video proved to be ineffective; it was too short to show what the program could do. After two months, it was dropped and prospects were offered a chance to see the whole package for a preview fee of $50.

After the demonstration video was dropped, the contents of these mailings cost approximately $3.50; postage ran another $2.40. Long distance charges averaged about $3 per prospect. Not only was this a low cost program, a shade under 1.5% of a gross sale, but the program could be conducted rapidly or slowly to control negative cash flow.

SELECTING
A MARKET

The Fortune 500 list seemed like the logical market segment from the outset. The Human Resources staff in these companies would be accustomed to buying high quality training and could appreciate the extra dimensions of a program designed by PhDs in communication. With multiple branches and locations, Fortune 500 companies would also offer a vast potential for multiple sales.

Small to mid-sized companies also looked like attractive prospects. They offered fewer chances for multiple sales, but also fewer purchasing committees and red tape. Quick decisions from a few small companies could rapidly change the cash flow from negative to positive.

To find the optimum market segment, Woolfson developed five prospect lists from the Thomas Register. For two-and-a-half months, two telemarketers went to the phone daily to make presentations followed by mailings to companies that grossed $1 million annually; $5 million annually; $10 million annually; $25 million annually and $50 million annually.

No company that was grossing less than $25 million showed any interest in the Negotiation and Bargaining Skills package. Even companies grossing $50 million a year were rarely interested enough to approve the $50 preview fee.

One tip-off to the sterility of these markets was the pattern of reasons given for lack of interest. Callers were repeatedly told "we don't use these programs"; "we don't train people in anything more than their work procedures"; "our factory workers aren't well enough educated to gain from these programs"; "we're too small." In the course of 200 phone contacts with owners and managers in these companies, it became obvious that these were valid reasons and not just put-downs aimed at telemarketers.

Another indication that companies in these market segments were unlikely prospects was that callers heard no suggestions on how the product package could be improved. Although they consistently advanced the idea that the program would be useful because "everybody needs to be a negotiator at all levels of their activities," the lack of interest was stifling. There are, of course, minor exceptions in any such pattern. Two companies paid to preview the program, and six months later one of these purchased the product package to train for one-on-one situations between managers and hourly wage personnel.

SUBCONTRACTING THE CAMPAIGN

Even before the first phone calls were made, Woolfson learned of three experienced telemarketers who were forming a small company. To get more hands on the phone, Woolfson negotiated a contract based on dividing sales commissions. He gave the new firm a set of prospect lists structured like those used at Woolfson and Company; the results were similar. In less than two months, the subcontractor and Woolfson terminated the contract by mutual agreement. Although long-term prospects remained bright, the program was painfully slow for the subcontractor, who needed a positive cash flow to survive.

PREPARING FOR
THE LONG HAUL

As soon as it was obvious companies grossing under $50 million showed little interest, Woolfson began laying the groundwork to shift to the Fortune 500 market. While compiling a new prospect list, he advised Fox and Barclay that success would require a long-term commitment.

Testing the Market: As we have said before, the only valid way to test a telephone market is to gather information while trying to sell the product, then step back and evaluate the results. The telemarketers did just that, targeting the Fortune 500 with the same approach they had tried with other companies.

Three months of contacts with Fortune 500 companies revealed these patterns:

1. From the outset, almost every prospect agreed to accept and read the printed material. In follow-up calls after the mailings, comments from most prospects indicated they had read what was sent. Thus, the campaign was successful in generating interest.

2. Approximately 33% of the prospects who reviewed the first packet of literature were interested enough to invest the $50 preview fee. This early response differed so markedly from the under $50 million companies it caused an overly optimistic projection of initial sales.

3. No one objected to the $600 price, which indicated it was acceptable.

4. No sales were closed, but the telemarketers picked up valuable marketing information. They learned the legitimate objections to the product and they discovered the buying schedules and patterns in the companies they were contacting.

5. The staff came to believe that, if they could establish strong relationships with a few directors of human resource development, they would be able to network among subsidiaries, affiliates, and other departments in these huge corporations. Eventually, large multiple sales of the product package would be feasible.

FINDING
DECISION-MAKERS

Working with receptionists in major corporations is an art in itself. As we would expect, receptionists in Fortune 500 companies are highly intelligent and above average in skills. However, they were often unable to direct the initial call to the right decision-maker. After some weeks, it became apparent the Woolfson and Company staff were complicating the problem.

They began using the obvious approach—find the person by title. Within a matter of weeks they had uncovered a glossary of titles for the same function—not only from company to company but from division to division within some companies. Initial long-distance costs ran high as each call was bumped through a series of three or four persons. Although many telemarketing types would label this "the old run-around," that would be a mistake. With more management positions, these giant companies had more titles and no standard pattern for assigning functions. Even insiders were sometimes confused.

The effort to find the right decision-maker improved dramatically when the staff abandoned titles and simply described the function. A telemarketer would say to the receptionist: "I need to talk with the person in charge of human resources training." With that description, the receptionist either knew who to put on the line, or came close enough so that whoever answered knew the decision-maker. This approach reduced phone bills 20% with an equal savings in staff time.

REFINING
THE PRODUCT

Although there was never a time from the outset of the Fortune 500 campaign when the initial presentation failed to stir further interest with the majority of prospects, sales remained insignificant for more than a year until Fox, Barclay, and Woolfson solved a basic problem in the description of the product.

In the beginning, they believed all six parts of the Negotiation and Bargaining Skills program represented basic skills, what the professors called a syntax level of training. Telemarketers described it as "a program for everybody."

Some of the tapes actually covered fairly advanced topics. When prospects discovered these advanced segments in the preview, they generally felt the program would not be suitable for average employees.

On the other hand, when the program was described as a curriculum for managers, department heads, and professionals, prospects felt it was too shallow to meet needs normally fulfilled with live workshops ranging from two to five days.

The Objections: After three months of Fortune 500 marketing, many companies had previewed the cassettes and reviewed the workbooks, but none had purchased the program. Uniformly they told the telemarketers that although it was an excellent program they could not buy it. Most frequently heard was: "We don't know how to fit this into our training plan. It's well done but. . .."

One prospect stated it well when he said: "It's good but it doesn't fill a pressing need. . . you know the kind of need that causes us to feel that we should have had it yesterday, and we're not going to let tomorrow dawn without having it."

Possible Changes: The dilemma had become painfully clear: the package appeared too shallow for managers but too deep for hourly workers, and training departments could not figure out how to make it fit their company's needs. Fox, Barclay, and Woolfson held a strategy session to consider alternatives. Woolfson asked if it would it be possible to edit and revise the video cassettes to meet specific requirements of the target market. Both time and funding ruled out that approach.

As another option, he suggested writing a battery of complex true/false, and multiple choice tests to aid retention and make it easier to fit the package into corporate training plans?

Adding Value: The professors agreed that development of the tests would be possible, and they asked Woolfson to be on their test writing team because of his exposure to needs expressed on the phone by the non-buying prospects.

The test battery consisted of several quizzes for each segment of the cassette—a total of 473 questions. As the telemarketing continued, it became apparent the test battery was a unique selling point. No other videotape vendor had anything to match it.

The Results: The telemarketers began stressing the value of the tests in every call. Interest levels on the other end of the phone line perked up considerably; the ratio of previewers climbed, and more important, some previewers bought the product.

REFINING
THE MAILING

The Brochure: At the same strategy meeting, the three men agreed on the need to create a brochure to add to the other material being mailed. The first brochure was ready almost as quickly as the test battery. The brochure story line started with the statement, "Negotiation Rules Are As Important As Grammar Rules," and it clearly defined the six parts of the program: "Fundamentals of Persuasion," "Inquiry Method," "Effective Influence Techniques," "Bargaining and Strategies," "Negotiator Style," and "Level Shifting." It explained why the program was developed; gave background information on the professors; explained the testing program; gave information on the preview rentals, and listed prices. Most of this information had been available in the letter or other material, but everyone agreed the compactness of the brochure gave it more punch.

Other Material: In addition to the brochure, the follow-up mailings now included an announcement of the program's bronze medal, a question and answer sheet addressing the concerns most frequently expressed by prospects, a sample test for one lecture, and an order blank.

Results: After the test battery and new follow-up mailing were integrated into the program, fewer than 10% of the prospects dropped out for lack of interest. Managers who indicated interest but did not buy became closely monitored long-term prospects. To maintain the business relationship, telemarketers called back at reasonable intervals. Some of these prospects became purchasers after more than a year of contact work.

EXPANDING
THE LINE

Adding Audio: Fifteen months after their original agreement, Fox asked Woolfson to evaluate a half-dozen audio cassettes made during a live workshop to determine whether they were marketable. Woolfson agreed with Fox's own assessment that with editing the audio cassettes could form the basis of a "train the trainer" program to be integrated with the video package. Together, they roughed out the entire "train the trainer" package: a syllabus with outlines of the audio lectures, cross references to the video program, and directions and handouts for the exercises used in the live workshops.

Unfortunately, Dr. Fox discovered that making needed changes in the rough cassettes made in the live workshop situation were more demanding than he anticipated. It took fully 15 months until the master set of professional fidelity audio cassettes was completed.

The New Price Structure: As the audio cassettes were being readied for market, Fox and Woolfson worked out a new set of incentives. A prospect who paid the $50 preview fee and liked the product could have that money applied to a $150 rental for a pilot workshop using the all the cassettes and related materials. If the pilot workshop was successful, the prospect could apply the $150 toward the purchase of the first unit. This incremental approach toward a full commitment turned some skittish prospects into paying customers.

Testing the Waters: In the long interval before the "train the trainer" package went into production, the telemarketers continued selling the original package. As they did so, they discussed the new program and noted the reactions. During the long gestation period for the new product, the telemarketing team learned that the instructor's audio cassette program could play a vital role in the marketing of the then slow-moving video package and it also had the potential of standing on its own as a separate product.

A simple description of the new program would elicit these typical reactions:

> "I want to know more about it and sample it as soon as it's available."

> "It's competitive."

> "I like its flexibility."

> "It's cost-effective."

> "We need something like that."

There was an obvious shift from the earlier comment: "It looks like a good program but we don't know how to make it fit."

The Complete Line: Relying on this new marketing data, Fox, Barclay, and Woolfson restructured the line into three distinct products. The first three cassettes from the original set became the Basic Program, priced at $350. The original six-cassette set, which included the three Basic Program cassettes, was relabeled the Advanced Program; the price remained $600. The audio cassettes and syllabus became the Instructor Training Program, priced at $400 when purchased separately or $200 when purchased with the Basic Program or the Advanced program. If a training administrator wanted only the syllabus, which contained sufficient material to build workshops without reference to any of the cassettes, the price was $100. Additional workbooks and test sets were also available.

The restructured line appeared to meet all the objections. Prospects who wanted something simple to show to large numbers of employees could get the Basic Program. Those who wanted a full-blown, live workshop for managers could put it together with the resources in the Advanced Program and the Instructor Training Program.

FURTHER REFINEMENTS

As the new product line took shape, Woolfson created several new printed pieces to allow a variety of approaches to clients.

The New Brochure: Similar to the old brochure in design and color, this one described 15 different ways the product line could meet specific user needs.

The Information Bulletin: At the option of the telemarketer, the best prospects could be sent a series of 14 Information Bulletins to maintain and build interest. The Bulletins contained information about how other clients were using the programs as well as tips on handling common negotiation situations. Many of the ideas for these Bulletins came from phone conversations with prospects.

Other Materials: Prospects who showed interest in instructor training but did not immediately purchase the program could be sent samples of two key syllabus pages and a seven minute audio tape excerpt from the Instructor Training Program. The same audio cassette was routinely sent to all companies that spent $50 to preview the video package and to all holdover prospects from the first stage of marketing before introduction of the new products.

EVALUATING THE RESULTS

As this chapter is being written (two and a half years after the initial conversation between Fox and Woolfson), the Winning Word series of negotiation tapes seems well on its way to becoming an established line in human resources training. Sales are still slow, but improving steadily, and user reactions are consistently positive. Several companies have expressed an interest in mass purchases.

It would be easy to credit the success to perseverance, but the real key was adaptation. Winning Word and Woolfson and Company could have persevered ten years trying to sell a six-cassette package to companies grossing less than $10 million annually and had nothing to show for it. They succeeded because they listened to what prospects said and made appropriate adjustments—first by shifting market segments, then by restructuring the product line.

This case history also illustrates the accessibility of huge markets in a telephone campaign. Even the smallest company can succeed in reaching the giants of industry if its product fills a genuine need, if its callers are professional and persistent in working through the bureaucratic maze, if it is flexible enough to adapt to prospects' objections, and if it is patient enough to stay in the market through a long buying cycle.

KEY POINTS

1. Managers should be constantly monitoring the marketing data that comes back in a telemarketing campaign. Reluctant prospects provide clues for restructuring the promotion, the product, or both.

2. Even a very small company can succeed in marketing to the Fortune 500. Doing so requires a good product and the ability to adapt to changing needs. Staying power is essential.

OVERCOMING INTERNAL OBJECTIONS

The traditional antipathy to telemarketing, which we described in Chapter One and alluded to elsewhere, can derail a program before it gets rolling. Any manager who is seriously contemplating adopting a telemarketing strategy must consider possible opposition and how to meet it.

Opposition can come from anywhere, and it can be covert instead of open. Consider these possibilities:

1. The owner feels telemarketing is an unproven novelty. He understands the need to change but is reluctant to commit significant resources to an unproven concept. Result: he insists on low salaries and vetoes requests for better equipment and training.

2. The head of the shipping department feels telemarketing is undignified. He is further annoyed because rush orders from the telemarketing crew come in randomly during the day instead of being conveniently grouped. (He is used to outside sales orders coming all at once, either the last thing in the afternoon or the first thing in the morning.) Result: he tells the shippers to fill all other orders first before bothering with telemarketing orders.

3. The people who take orders by phone (sometimes called Inside Sales) hate telemarketing because it increases their workload. (Customers phone in orders now instead of giving them to a traveling representative.) Result: the order-takers refuse to be enlisted as telemarketers; snub anyone who does telemarketing; and sometimes refuse to take orders, suggesting the customer call a telemarketing representative instead.

4. The outside sales representatives see telemarketing as an evil force that cheats them out of commissions, degrades their profession, and threatens their way of life. Result: they bad mouth the new system to customers, refuse to cooperate with (or passively resist) telemarketers picking up converted accounts, and do everything possible to make telemarketers into second-class citizens.

5. The director of marketing worries about the reactions of his outside sales force. When they are upset, the sales figures drop. To keep them pacified, he delays converting accounts which could more logically be handled by telemarketing.

6. The head of computer operations may object to giving telemarketers access to the customer database or, alternately, may object to setting up separate telemarketing software. Result: he withholds information, so telemarketers don't know enough to use the computer tools.

For some people, telemarketing seems a radical move. If a manager understands that attitude, she can act to soften the opposition. While a book like this cannot cover all the possible situations, we suggest these general steps:

1. Get everyone involved in planning. Anyone with a stake in the program should have an input into how it will operate.

2. Listen for comments that indicate opposition or reluctance. Try to get objections out in the open where they can be resolved.

3. Avoid battles over turf. Remind combatants that when the company benefits, everyone benefits. The lower cost and bet-

ter customer service offered by telemarketing can make the company more competitive.

4. Offer positions in the new operation to anyone who is qualified. Maybe the obstinate outside salesman really would enjoy working on the phone.

5. Settle the question of how the sales function can best be organized and *then* consider how commissions are to be divided between various sales staffs.

6. After carefully evaluating objections and explaining the advantages of the changes, if opponents are relentless, consider transfering or releasing them.

"Be prepared" and "be patient" should be the watchwords of anyone introducing telemarketing into an established organization. The experience of thousands of companies indicates the transition may be stormy, but the advantages make it worth the trouble.

CONTRACTING FOR OUTSIDE TELEMARKETING

After carefully considering all the options, some companies choose to contract with an outside telemarketing firm rather than setting up an in-house operation. Before making that choice, however, a company needs to examine its reasons and make some tough decisions about the contract. An ill-conceived contracted campaign can fail just as easily as an ill-conceived in-house campaign. Success depends on good planning.

WHY CONTRACT?

Telemarketing, like most other functions, will be more expensive if contracted out. Other considerations, as these examples show, can make an outside contract the best option.

Short-Term Need: Matt Steiner quit his job as Chief Financial Officer of an industrial firm to become a full-time professional speaker and consultant. He speaks at conventions, conducts on-site workshops for clients, and consults with firms on investment strategy. He has hired an office coordinator to process direct mail, handle the phone and books, and control the calendar for his engagements.

He has been independent for two years and the business has been growing; during the second year he still sold fewer than half of the available days on his calendar, but he enjoyed a high percentage of repeat business and referrals. He can reasonably expect that once his calendar is full it will remain full as referrals increase. His immediate challenge is to double his paid dates to fill the calendar for next year.

Steiner's previous promotional efforts (direct mail and paid advertising) are successful, but slow. His operation needs a temporary boost after which direct mail and calls to old clients should be enough to maintain the momentum. He should consider hiring an outside firm to develop leads for several months. Then he or the office coordinator could follow-up and close the bookings. (Since Steiner himself is the product, he would be the most effective closer.)

Short-term needs for other firms might be the introduction of a new product, the penetration of a new market, or a seasonal opportunity. If a temporary boost is all that's needed, hiring and training a telemarketing staff would be overkill.

Keeping the Workforce Small: TopGuard is a small company which applies sealant to commercial and industrial roofs to stop leaks and extend the life of each roof. The owner believes he could expand by offering the sealant as preventive maintenance through an ongoing telemarketing campaign.

Despite good wages and reasonable working conditions, Top-Guard has chronic problems with absenteeism, turnover, and poor quality control, both on the work sites and in the office. The company is in a declining area with a poorly trained and shrinking labor pool. Contracting out will eliminate the need for adding employees with all the associated headaches (interviews, social security and workmen's comp., etc.).

Controlling Cash Flow: Trusty Rent-a-car is one of four car rental agencies operating from the airport in a city of 200,000. Most of the rentals are to travelers, with a few being temporary replacements for damaged cars. Most of these are paid by the insurance company. The manager wants to significantly expand the insurance rental segment of her business, but to do so she will need a permanent telemarketing program with periodic calls to body shops and insurance agencies.

Because the cash flow fluctuates from month to month, she hesitates adding another employee. As an alternative, she could contract with an outside firm, which would let her increase or decrease the telemarketing effort as conditions dictated.

Keeping the Company's Focus: Leo Ricci of Ricci Box Company knows some manufacturing firms in his area are buying packaging from out of state. He believes he can take away this business with a concerted effort.

Ricci Box has succeeded because supervisors and workers concentrated on what they do best: designing and mass-producing packaging. Leo would prefer to keep this focus by staying specialized. Therefore, he contracts for every service not closely related to making boxes.

CHOOSING THE CONTRACTOR

Picking the right contractor for a particular program requires considerable forethought.

Defining the Need: What are the objectives and what exactly do you want the contractor to do? Will the contract telemarketers actually close sales or just find leads? Will the contractor have to develop a prospect list? What pace is appropriate (how many people on the phones)? How long will the campaign last?

Finding Contractors: For local telemarketing firms, look in the telephone directory. National firms frequently advertise in industry publications such as *Telemarketing*. That magazine also prints periodically a Service Agency Roundup listing firms which "carry out a variety of telemarketing functions for clients." In talking with representatives of different contractors, remember no firm will be equally strong across the board. Look for firms which agree with your company's marketing philosophy and have experience with campaigns similar to the one you propose. Ask for references with needs similar to yours. Notice the impressions you get over the phone when talking with the contractor; prospects will get the same impression of your company.

Arranging Compensation: Most reputable firms will discuss your needs at some length without charge. If on-site visits or a lot of homework is involved, they may expect a preliminary consulting fee.

The basic contract can be priced in various ways. Some firms will have a fixed price schedule; others will negotiate. Some possibilities:

1. Set price per lead. This arrangement can tempt a contractor to turn in poorly qualified leads. To lessen the temptation, consider a guarantee (X percent of the leads will generate sales or the contractor pays a penalty). Another approach is to insist on good written records for each lead and then spot-check them.

2. An hourly rate or charge per contact. In this case compensation is tied to effort, not to results. This type of contract offers security to the contractor, which, presumably, will mean less pressure and more rapport with customers. Such a contract needs to be monitored closely. A lot of hours or a lot of contacts with no sales means someone should take a close look at the whole operation.

3. Straight commission. This is the type of contract Woolfson and Company had to sell the Winning Word negotiation tapes. This approach ties compensation directly to performance and appears to put all the risk on the telemarketer, but it has potential problems. If a big project does not turn a fast profit, the telemarketing firm could face serious cash flow problems and be forced to back out (as Woolfson's subcontractor did). Or they could slow the negative cash flow by putting this project on the back burner, making a few calls each month while concentrating on more profitable contracts. Unless there are extenuating circumstances, (such as a tight operating budget) we recommend dividing the risk.

4. Monthly fee plus commissions. In this method the contractor is asking the client company to share some of the risk. If the fee is high and the commission low, the client is in fact paying the equivalent of a salary and an incentive bonus. Because the telemarketing firm has some measure of security, they are unlikely to drop a project prematurely. Nor or they likely to plod through call after call without results.

5. Project pricing. A telemarketing firm might offer a full package including research, list development, brochure design and printing, direct mail, qualifying leads, handling inbound calls and taking orders, and writing a report on the results. This arrangement greatly simplifies things from the client's viewpoint, but it involves a significant financial commitment with no guarantee of success. Anyone considering such an arrangement should check the telemarketer's track record for every proposed activity. Just because a firm does well on the phone does not necessarily mean its people understand brochure design.

MAKING THE PARTNERSHIP WORK

Having the right words on paper does not guarantee the project will succeed. A smart manager will keep in close contact with the telemarketers, review the results frequently, and stay flexible in case a mid-course correction is needed.

RECOMMENDED READING

Cathcart, Jim. *Relationship Selling.* (New York, NY: Perigee Books, 1990).

Dudley, George W. and Goodson, Shannon L. *The Psychology of Call Reluctance: How to Overcome the Fear of Self-Promotion.* (Dallas, TX: Behavioral Science Research Press, 1986).

Fidel, Stanley Leo. *Start-Up Telemarketing: How to Launch a Profitable Sales Operation.* (New York, NY: John Wiley, 1987).

Fisher, Peg. *Successful Telemarketing: A Step-By-Step Guide For Increased Sales at Lower Cost.* (Chicago, IL: Dartnell Corporation, 1985).

"Industrywide Software Roundup." *Telemarketing,* June 1990, pp. 48-65.

Kauffman, Ronald S. *Future$ell: Automating Your Sales Force.* (Boulder, CO: Cross Communications, 1990).

Lauderbach, Bill. "The Well-Appointed Work Place." *Telemarketing,* September 1990, pp. 82-85.

LeBoeuf, Michael. *How To Win Customers and Keep Them For Life.* (New York, NY: Berkley Books, 1987).

Linchitz, Joel. *The Complete Guide to Telemarketing Management.* (New York, NY: AMACOM, 1990).

Lipman, Andrew D. "Telemarketing Enforcement on the Rise." *Telemarketing,* June 1990, pp. 10-13.

Mahfood, Phillip E. *Teleselling: High Performance Business to Business Phone Selling Techniques.* (Chicago, IL: Probus Publishing, 1990).

Masi, Kathy and Bates, Connie. "Generating Sales Leads With Telemarketing." *Telemarketing,* July 1990, pp. 40-42.

McCafferty, Thomas. *In-House Telemarketing: A Masterplan for Starting and Managing a Profitable Telemarketing Program.* (Chicago, IL: Probus Publishing, 1987).

McInerney, Lori. "'No Tears' Telephone Marketing." *IN-BOUND/OUTBOUND,* September 1990, pp. 28-33.

Newton, Harry. "Think Database." *INBOUND/OUTBOUND,* September 1990, pp. 69-75.

Tehrani, Nadji. "Fax + Phone = The Most Explosive Marketing Tool." *Telemarketing,* June 1990, p. 1.

"ABC's 20/20 Telemarketing Coverage—Unfair and Outrageously One-Sided!" *Telemarketing,* July 1990, pp. 40-42.

Walther, George R. *Phone Power: How To Make the Telephone Your Most Profitable Business Tool.* (New York, NY: Berkley Books, 1986).

INDEX

ABOUT THE AUTHORS

Raymond C. Harlan is president of ComSkills, where he teaches and develops workshops on communication and management skills.

Walter M. Woolfson, Jr. spent over forty years in journalism and telemarketing prior to his death in 1988.

Additional Titles in
The Entrepreneur's Guide Series
Available from Probus Publishing

How to Sell Your Business for the Best Price (With the Least Worry!), Vaughn Cox

Entrepreneur's Guide to Capital, Revised Edition, Jennifer Lindsey

Forecasting Your Company's Sales and Profits (Quickly, Easily and Realistically!), Kenneth E. Marino

Cashflow, Credit and Collection: Over 100 Proven Techniques for Protecting and Strengthening Your Balance Sheet, Basil P. Mavrovitis

Funding Research & Development: How to Team Up with the Federal Government to Finance Your R & D, Patrick D. O'Hara

Initial Public Offerings: All You Need to Know About Taking a Company Public, David P. Sutton and M. William Benedetto

Mastering the Business Cycle: How to Keep Your Company on Track in Times of Economic Change, Albert N. Link

Negotiating a Bank Loan (You Can Live With!), Arthur G. Pulis III

Crafting the Perfect Name: The Art and Science of Naming a Company or Product, George Burroughs Blake and Nancy Blake-Bohné

Acquisitions: How to Expand, Extend and Defend Your Business, Sharon L. Blanding

Building a Winning Sales Team: How to Recruit, Train and Motivate the Best, Gini Graham Scott

Forthcoming Titles

How to Export: Everything You Need to Know to Get Started, Roger Fritz